The Assistant Principal'

Though traditionally responsible for school operations, assistant principals increasingly find themselves expected to provide academic leadership as students face a growing emphasis on academic performance. This timely book helps current and aspiring assistant principals implement best practices for their evolving roles, providing the knowledge and skills required to succeed in their schools. Coverage includes:

- Emphasis on competency-based leadership requirements
- Research-based models, tips, snapshots, best-practices, and recommendations
- Unique discussion of the assistant principal as a student advocate
- Organizational strategies, professional growth activities, and operational models for program implementation
- Specific leadership responsibilities for school climate, personnel administration, professional development, and performance appraisal
- Case studies and discussion questions to foster applied learning

Dr. M. Scott Norton is a former public school teacher, coordinator of curriculum, assistant superintendent, and superintendent of schools. He has served as professor and vice-chair of the Department of Educational Administration at the University of Nebraska at Lincoln and as professor and chair of the Department of Educational Administration at Arizona State University where he is currently professor emeritus.

The Principal as Human Resources Leader
A Guide to Exemplary Practices for Personnel Administration
M. Scott Norton

The Principal as Student Advocate
A Guide for Doing What's Best for All Students
M. Scott Norton, Larry K. Kelly, and Anna R. Battle

**Great Assistant Principals and the (Great) Principals
  Who Mentor Them**
A Practical Guide
Carole Goodman and Christopher Berry

Solving the Assistant Principal's Puzzle
Douglas Hartley

The Principal as Instructional Leader
A Practical Handbook, Third Edition
Sally J. Zepeda

Leading Schools in an Era of Declining Resources
J. Howard Johnston and Ronald Williamson

The School Leader's Guide to Formative Assessment
Using Data to Improve Student and Teacher Achievement
Todd Stanley and Jana Alig

The School Leader's Guide to Social Media
Ronald Williamson and J. Howard Johnston

Data Analysis for Continuous School Improvement
Third Edition
Victoria Bernhardt

The Trust Factor
Strategies for School Leaders
Julie Peterson Combs, Stacey Edmonson, and Sandra Harris

What Great Principals Do Differently
18 Things That Matter Most, Second Edition
Todd Whitaker

Creating Safe Schools
A Guide for School Leaders, Teachers, and Parents
Franklin P. Schargel

The Assistant Principal's Guide

New Strategies for New Responsibilities

M. Scott Norton

Routledge
Taylor & Francis Group

NEW YORK AND LONDON

First published 2015
by Routledge
711 Third Avenue, New York, NY 10017

and by Routledge
2 Park Square, Milton Park, Abingdon, Oxon, OX14 4RN

Routledge is an imprint of the Taylor & Francis Group, an informa business

© 2015 Taylor & Francis

The right of M. Scott Norton to be identified as author of this work has been asserted by him in accordance with sections 77 and 78 of the Copyright, Designs and Patents Act 1988.

Library of Congress Cataloging-in-Publication Data
Norton, M. Scott.
   The assistant principal's guide : new strategies for new responsibilities /
M. Scott Norton.
      pages cm
   Includes bibliographical references and index.
   1. Assistant school principals—United States.   2. School management and organization—United States.   I. Title.
LB2831.92.N638 2014
371.2′012—dc23
2014025549

ISBN: 978-1-138-81463-9 (hbk)
ISBN: 978-1-138-81466-0 (pbk)
ISBN: 978-1-315-74731-6 (ebk)

Typeset in Bembo and Helvetica Neue
by Apex CoVantage, LLC

Contents

Meet the Author

M. Scott Norton, a former public school teacher, coordinator of curriculum, assistant superintendent and superintendent of schools, served as Professor and Vice-Chair of the Department of Educational Administration and Supervision at the University of Nebraska, Lincoln, later becoming Professor and Chair of the Department of Educational Administration and Policy Studies at Arizona State University, where he is currently Professor Emeritus. His primary graduate teaching areas include classes in human resources administration, school superintendency, school principalship, educational leadership and competency-based administration.

Dr. Norton is the author of college textbooks in the areas of human resources administration and the school superintendency, and has co-authored other books on the school principal as a student advocate, the school principal as a learning leader, and administrative management. He has published widely in national journals in such areas as teacher retention, teacher load, retention of quality school principals, organizational climate, support personnel in schools, employee assistance programs, distance education, and others. One of his latest textbooks, *Competency-based Leadership: A Guide for High Performance in the Role of School Principal*, was published by Rowman and Littlefield Education in 2013. His book, *The School Principal as Human Resources Leader*, is currently in press.

He has received several state and national awards honoring his services and contributions to the field of educational administration from such organizations as the American Association of School Administrators, the University Council for Educational Administrators, the Arizona School Administrators Association, the Arizona Educational Research Organization, Arizona State University College of Education Dean's Award for excellence in service to the field, and the distinguished service award from the Arizona Education Information Service.

Dr. Norton's state and national leadership positions have included service as Executive Director of the Nebraska Association of School Administrators, a member of the Board of Directors for the Nebraska Congress of Parents and Teachers, President of the Nebraska Council of Teachers of Mathematics, President of the Arizona School Administrators Higher Education Division, Arizona School Administrators Board of Directors, Staff Associate of the University Council for School Administrators, Treasurer for the University Council for School Administrators, and Nebraska State Representative for the National Association of Secondary School Principals. He also has served on the Board of Editors for the American Association of School Public Relations.

Preface

The administrative role of a school's assistant principal historically has been centered on one general responsibility, that of "assisting the school principal in the overall administration of the school program and operations of the campus and to coordinate assigned activities and services." But just what specific administrative responsibilities are assigned to the role of assistant principal and just how the role relates to the present demands for instructional leadership are not always clear. As noted by Glanz (2004), duties of assistant principals are primarily assigned by the school principal and doing so often leads to role ambiguity and conflicts in understanding what the assistant principal role really is. For this reason, although the book centers on the changing role of the assistant principal, it also addresses the necessary leadership of the school principal in changing and improving the role of the assistant principal.

Assistant principals commonly have been viewed as persons in charge of student discipline and other management roles such as crisis management, bus scheduling, lunchroom supervision, and other such duties as assigned by the school principal. In most cases, the work of the assistant principal has been only tangentially related to the primary responsibilities of a practicing school principal. With the advent of demands for improved academic performance on the part of all students and the accompanying demands for accountability, new leadership skills and competencies have emerged for school assistant principals. The new calls for improved academic performance have been accompanied by requirements for leadership in other administrative functions as well, including human resources administration, pupil personnel administration, and programs such as special education, student advocacy, competency-based administration, and school law.

The Primary Purpose of the Book

The primary purpose of the book is to provide assistant principals, principals, and aspiring individuals with the knowledge, skills and understandings that loom important for successful practices in the role of assistant principal. In addition, school principals who are looking for direction in the assignment of responsibilities for their assistant principal(s) will find the book of special value. Members of college/university faculties that prepare school administrators will find the book especially relevant in such courses as the school principalship, administrative leadership, school organizational development, the assistant school principal, competency-based administration, personnel administration, and others.

The text underscores the fact that current programs of preparation for assistant principals fall short of meeting contemporary needs. Merely trying to learn the responsibilities of an assistant school principal on the job is an unsatisfactory answer to meeting the many contemporary challenges facing the role. Simply examining what assistant principals do presently is unsatisfactory as well. The need is to study and analyze the immediate and future program requirements for student learning and then set administrative position descriptions and identify primary tasks and competencies required to accomplish them. This book not only provides recommendations for implementing best practices for assistant principals' leadership roles, but sets forth recommend changes for the role that are intended to place the assistant principal in a learning leadership position.

It is true that position descriptions for assistant principals at the high school level are trending toward specializations. That is, a larger high school might have four or even five assistant principals, one in charge of athletics, one in charge of student personnel, one in charge of curriculum, one in charge of activities, and one serving as the school's registrar. The book presents examples of position descriptions representative of those needed in practice. However, the concept of specialization is becoming more and more evident in the position descriptions for assistant principals at every level of school operations. Keep in mind that many schools, especially at the elementary school level, still do not have assistant principals—a serious oversight in education in America's schools today.

The Need for Improved Position Strategies for Assistant Principals

As noted by Glanz (1994), "the research available on their role (assistant principals) and responsibilities is extremely limited." Unfortunately, the responsibilities of assistant principals continue to be somewhat nebulous and unstructured. Although position descriptions of assistant principals commonly list responsibilities such as "assisting the school principal in the general administration of the school," just what the assistant principal does in this regard is not sufficiently defined.

Research and empirical evidence have underscored the fact that preparation programs for assistant principals have not been satisfactory. School principals have had to assume new instructional leadership roles to meet the demands for improved student academic achievement. The increasing workload for school principals necessitates the need for additional support services in planning, implementing, coordinating and evaluating improved programs for student learning. There is a growing need for school principals to delegate various aspects of instructional leadership to other qualified school leaders.

In addition, the managerial duties of the assistant principal have not been instrumental in providing experience in the area of instructional leadership. Thus, the specific leadership role of the assistant principal at any level of school operations remains unclear. The book focuses on this problem and recommends organizational strategies, professional growth activities, competency, knowledge and skills requirements for successful performance in the position of assistant principal, best practices and operational models for program implementation. The lists of skills, competencies and indicators of competencies for the assistant school principal in the book are to serve as standards for a school to work toward rather than ones that should be performed in all schools at all organizational levels.

Best Empirical Practices and Research Support

For several years the author and a professional colleague have conducted administrative workshops for assistant school principals and those educators who aspire to the position of assistant principal. Best practices and needs for improving the authority and leadership of assistant school principals as instructional leaders were included in the program.

Personal interviews with practicing school principals and assistant principals were completed prior to the submission of this book proposal. Interviews centered on the perceptions of the interviewees about current work responsibilities of assistant principals and recommendations for needed changes/improvements in the position of assistant school principal. A survey of school assistant principals also was completed, asking for their judgment as to the importance of nine administrative tasks (e.g., role as instructional leader, role in personnel administration, role in student safety and welfare, role in management activities such as budgeting, scheduling, busing, etc., role in supervision of support personnel, and others).

Organization of the Text

The book is presented in six chapters that address the primary responsibilities and best practices of assistant principals. Chapter 1 emphasizes the changing priorities of school goals and the demands for bringing relevance to the assistant principal's leadership role. These changes bring about new responsibilities of the local school principal and, in turn, the need for additional professional support on the part of the school's assistant principal. Chapter 2 focuses on the important concept of competency-based leadership and the new skills and knowledge needed by assistant principals to develop contemporary school learning cultures. The chapter emphasizes the importance of developing meaningful standards for the role of assistant principal in order to establish the importance of this leadership position. Chapter 3 centers on the unique topic of the assistant school principal as a student advocate. What is a student advocate and what does this concept mean in regard to the effectiveness of an assistant principal on the job? Chapter 4 views the assistant principal in his or her changing role as a learning leader, and Chapter 5 follows with an in-depth discussion of leadership for the growing area of student personnel services. Chapter 6 is a resource file that sets forth standards and related knowledge and skills required on the part of assistant principals in contemporary schools. As will be noted in the special features section that follows, each chapter begins by stating the chapter's primary goal. A summary closes each chapter and is followed by a set of discussion questions that foster extended learning opportunities for the reader. In addition, case studies accompany each chapter. In these studies, the reader is asked to assume the role of an assistant principal and respond administratively to the matter at hand. A comprehensive reference list is also included in each chapter.

Special Features of the Book

The book addresses the primary responsibilities of the school assistant principal by:

1. Viewing the role of the competency-based assistant school principal as a school leader in a learning-centered school as opposed to serving primarily as a management administrator.
2. Providing examples of best practices related to the work of the assistant school principal in each chapter of the book.
3. Presenting research and empirical concepts and models of successful practices of effective leadership on the part of assistant principals in the primary areas of work responsibilities.
4. Emphasizing the major tasks of assistant school principals and illustrating just how these tasks can be successfully implemented in practice.
5. Placing emphasis on the academic leadership that must be provided by the assistant principal in serving the goals and objectives determined by the school principal and members of the school's professional and classified staff.
6. Placing an emphasis on students and their academic achievement through such administrative leadership as being a true student advocate.

7. Emphasizing such major topics as school climate, personnel administration, professional growth and development, performance appraisal, and others that loom important in realizing improved student achievement and goal achievement.

8. Using a reader-friendly writing style that encourages the reader to participate in the "quizzes," "snapshots," "lightbulb experiences," and exercises that are appropriately included in several chapters.

9. Emphasizing the importance of the assistant principal's leadership role in contemporary school programming; supporting the need for qualified assistant principals to remedy the continuous increase of work responsibilities on the part of the modern day school principal.

10. Encouraging those persons who aspire to administrative roles in education to give full consideration to entering the position of assistant principal and assuming the important challenges faced in that leadership role.

11. Emphasizing the importance of the school principal becoming knowledgeable of the changes needed in the assignments of assistant principals in order for them to become effective leaders in accomplishing the mission of the school.

References

Glanz, J. (1994). Redefining the role of the assistant principal. *The Clearing House*, 67(5), 283–287.

Glanz, J. (2004). *The Assistant Principal's Handbook: Strategies for Success*. Thousand Oaks, CA: Sage.

The Assistant School Principal

Bringing This Leadership Position to Life!

Primary chapter goal:

To underscore the need for positive changes in the role of the assistant school principal for meeting present and future school goals and objectives.

You have most likely played the game of word relationships whereby someone says certain words and you respond immediately with the first word or thought that comes to mind. OK, ready? What word comes to mind when you think of the word, **assistant principal**? _____. Did you perhaps say disciplinarian, principal's helper, it all depends—or did you just go blank in search of an answer? Don't be surprised to learn that the role of the assistant school principal has been somewhat nebulous since 1839 when head assistants were hired in a few schools to serve under the principal-teacher (Pierce, 1935). At this early date, school principals, sometimes called headmasters, commonly taught in the classroom as well as taking care of administrative duties. The primary responsibility of the head assistants was to replace the school principal when he was teaching. Although the position of assistant school principal has been established in schools nationally, there are still many schools, especially at the elementary school level, that do not have assistant principals on the staff. Through the 1950s and 1960s, many elementary schools still had school principals who served part time as classroom teachers. And today, many elementary schools in the nation still do not employ an assistant principal.

Empirical evidence suggests that all too many schools that do have assistant principals do not have meaningful roles for them to play. This chapter underscores the seriousness of the lack of purpose in the assistant principal's position

1

responsibilities today, and the following chapters discuss specific ideas as to what must be done to bring the assistant school principal to life. Research has found that school principals are the ones who determine the responsibilities of assistant principals in their schools. It is for this reason that the information in this guide is of special importance for the school principal as well as for assistant principals and those who aspire to the role of assistant principal. The school principal commonly hires the assistant principal, establishes the responsibilities for the assistant principal, supervises and evaluates the assistant principal, and serves as a mentor for the assistant principal(s) in his or her school.

Changing Times and New Educational Demands for School Principals

The lack of retention of quality school principals continues to be an inhibiting factor in efforts to improve educational outcomes in schools nationally. The work responsibilities of the nation's school principals have increased continuously over the last several decades due to internal and external increases in job requirements, demands for program performance accountability, ongoing changes of mandates to meet curriculum/achievement standards, the diversification of the student population and community populations that must be served, and the reluctance of licensed personnel willing to help meet these challenges. In one study, the increasing demands on the work life of school principals was named as the number one reason for their leaving or considering leaving their present position as principal (Norton, 2002). In addition, the increasing demands for accountability within the principal's role have decreased the interest of other educators to aspire to the principalship as a professional career. "Within the mandate for school reform and instructional leadership, there is recognition that one person is not capable of performing all the roles traditionally prescribed to the school principal, yet the significance of the assistant's role is not given import" (Dunleavy, 2011, p. 9).

Foundational Factors That Underscore the Need for Effective Principal Support

Several factors underscoring the need for additional principal support are set forth in the following summary:

1. "Expectations for the principalship have steadily expanded since the reforms of the early 1980's, always adding to, and never subtracting from, the job description" (Copland, 2001, p. 4). Work life considerations have loomed important for those persons in this leadership position.

2. "If there is an all-encompassing challenge for school leaders, it is to lead the transition from the bureaucratic model of schooling with its emphasis on minimal levels of education for many, to a post industrial, adaptive model, with the goal of educating all youngsters well" (NASSP, "Changing Role of the Middle Level and High School Leader," 2007, p. 3).

3. "School leaders today must serve as leaders for student learning" (Institute for Educational Leadership, 2000). School principals are working under the mandates of NCLB (No Child Left Behind), as well as related state requirements to meet prescribed student achievement standards, in order to avoid the sanctions that are possible under Title I funding. Student testing requirements, academic achievement standards, and teacher performance assessments and evaluations serve to control much of the school principal's administrative time.

Academic performance standards for students are required by federal agencies, state departments and local school boards. Such standards, in some cases, are changed from year to year; principals are placed in a quandary in their efforts to change procedures that were only recently initiated.

4. External interventions and flawed mandates inhibit effective practices. Although we encourage efforts on the part of school leaders to stand strong for policies that favor student achievement, they have yet to be able to take strong stands against various external policy recommendations that are injurious to the best interests of students. Politically, their hands most often are tied to stand and confront such issues. Nevertheless, a true student advocate must have the courage to speak against flawed policies and recommendations that are damaging rather than helpful to students.

5. Empirical and research evidence resulting from limited study of the assistant school principal's position reveals that the work responsibilities frequently are spasmodic and loosely tied to the real tasks that principals must perform in practice. In such instances, the need for quality succession to the position of school principal is inhibited.

6. The roles for school principals are changing from authoritative and controlling approaches to positive relational approaches that serve to empower others through various methods of distributive leadership. Knowledge and skills that center on learning leadership and the implementation of distributive leadership are needed, as opposed to managing and controlling people and programs.

7. The preparation programs for practice in educational administration have not always centered on student learning and achievement strategies. Rather, such courses as school finance, supervision, school facilities planning, school law, policy and regulation development, school organization, guidance, and other management courses were part of their preparation programs. Curriculum and

instructional leadership work commonly was included in one course of supervision. The one course on the school principal commonly considered the work of school principals at all three levels of instruction: elementary, junior high/middle school, and secondary. In most programs, the study of the assistant school principalship is completely neglected.

It is not that the courses in the foregoing paragraph are not of relevance to school administration, rather the preparation program for school administrators most often has not placed an emphasis on student achievement and the fostering of a learning culture within the school.

8. Just as former president Harry Truman's desk plate indicated that "The buck stops here," that statement now applies to the desk of the school principal. Accountability for purposeful educational outcomes rests with the school principal. Hard data are being required as evidence to prove educational gains and improvements. Assessment and evaluation skills loom more important than ever before. Tying academic program outcomes to meeting the goals and purposes of the school's existence leads the list of the principal's responsibilities. No school principal has a "magic wand" that brings about student academic performance automatically. New knowledge, skills and competency are required on the part of the school leaders.

9. The need for new knowledge and skills on the part of the school principal relative to developing a learning culture in the school requires an ongoing program of professional growth and development. School principals are required to be involved continuously in improving their own administrative competence. Being told "what to do" is seldom accompanied by "how to accomplish it." Competency-based performance requires the achievement of new skills and knowledge on an ongoing basis. This topic is considered later in Chapter 2.

10. Current trends include the delegation of certain educational functions from the central school district office to the local school. Instructional leadership represents one such function. However, other functions of paramount importance for effective education outcomes also are finding their way to the principal's office. Human resources administration, supervision of the classified/support staff, marketing of the school's program, and meeting the demands for accountability through evidence of hard data are among other administrative functions that must be attended to at the local school level.

The foregoing contentions are examples of changes in the school principal's position that underscore the need for the school's assistant principal to be a position that is instrumental in providing the kind of leadership that serves to accomplish the school's mission. We submit that such a goal will not be accomplished without making significant changes in the role, authority and qualifications of the assistant school principal, and professional growth programs that center on the knowledge and skills required by a relevant position description.

We are not proposing that the assistant principal completely assume many of the responsibilities of the school principal. Rather, the assistant principal must be given increased involvement in the primary functions of the school. Only by assigning the assistant principal meaningful responsibilities for the primary functions of the school can the position be enhanced and the school benefited by the services of the assistant principal's position.

The Evolution of the Assistant School Principal

Attempting to identify the beginning of assistant principals in school administration is difficult at best. We do know that positions such as assistant teachers, head assistant, and even positions of grammar master and writing master were early historical assignments whereby one person was assigned to assist the school principal or head master by taking charge of the principal's classroom when he/she was visiting other rooms, keeping good discipline, carrying out instructional duties, and being second in command when the principal was away. For example, by 1839 head assistants took charge when the principal was attending to other administrative tasks. By 1857, a principal and head assistant assumed joint responsibility for a school in Boston. In 1864, head assistants were appointed to several schools and other teachers were hired to assume the classroom duties previously performed by the head assistants.

The addition of assistant school principals at the secondary school level increased gradually from 1945 to 1965. Nevertheless, during these two decades many schools nationally, especially elementary schools, did not have the services of an assistant principal. It is not unusual to have part-time assistant principals in America's schools even today.

Today, almost every middle and high school has the services of one or more assistant school principals. Such is not the case for elementary schools. We support the administrative models that include a school principal or co-principals with the administrative support of department/grade-level chairs, and assistant principals. In addition, we strongly recommend the use of teacher-leaders for administrative support in their areas of strength. The distributive administrative leadership organization will serve as the focus of the following book chapters.

A Pre-Quiz on the Assistant School Principal's Position

Take a few minutes to test your knowledge of a few of the conditions surrounding the role of principal and assistant principal in America's schools today. Check your answer for each of the statements that follow. Refrain from just guessing the answer; if you really do not know the answer, just move on to the next question.

1. Empirical evidence indicates that school districts throughout the country are facing problems and unprecedented challenges in recruiting and retaining competent school administrators. True ____ or False ____.

2. As late as the 1960s, many elementary school districts nationally had school principals who taught part-time as classroom teachers. True ____ or False ____.

3. In one study, three-fourths of the school principals reported that they did not need assistant principals to fulfill the expanding role of the principalship; they could handle these tasks themselves. True ____ or False ____.

4. The median annual salary of school principals in 2014 in the U.S. was $95,336. The median salary of assistant school principals the same year was approximately one-half that of school principals. True ____ or False ____.

5. One of the primary reasons that the responsibilities of the assistant school principal have been nebulous and undefined is that the specific tasks and related competencies needed by assistant principals have never been studied and reported. True ____ or False ____.

6. Although the role of the assistant school principal has yet to be validated in practice, one of the "most researched" and discussed roles in educational leadership is that of the assistant principal. True ____ or False ____.

7. A positive finding in the large majority of studies of the assistant principal is that experience in the role does give them a "good foundation" for entering and implementing the role of principal. True ____ or False ____.

8. Despite declining enrollments in many schools due to the advent of charter schools, increased home schooling practices, e-classes and other educational outlets, for public relations and political reasons, school leaders are advised to refrain from "marketing their school" or entering the world of politics in order to compete for student enrollments. True ____ or False ____.

9. One of the most cited studies on the role and responsibilities of the assistant school principal was conducted by Austin and Brown in 1970. The study found that the school principal commonly assigned the duties of the assistant principal without reference to a specific job description. True ____ or False ____.

10. In the overwhelming number of research studies on the work of the assistant school principal, the task of being an academic learning leader commonly is listed as their number one job responsibility. True ____ or False ____.

Answers to the foregoing pre-quiz are as follows: (1) T, (2) T, (3) F, (4) F, (5) F, (6) F, (7) F, (8) F, (9) T, (10) F. Now, let's briefly discuss each of the questions posed in the pre-quiz. Scoreboard: 10–8 correct, excellent; 7–5 correct, good; 4–2 correct, fair; 1–0 correct, read the following section and then retake the quiz.

Quiz Discussion—Let's Consider the Answers to the Pre-Quiz

True and False Statements

Statement #1 is true. Evidence provided in the literature and statements by school district personnel throughout the United States are expressing the problem of recruiting, hiring and retaining qualified school principals. Some sources indicate that there is a sufficient number of licensed educators to fill principal vacancies, but many licensed persons do not choose to enter the principalship as a career.

Statement #2 is true. Unfortunately, even today in some elementary schools, the school principal continues to teach part-time. Historical data concerning the number of schools in America with part-time principals are not readily available, "Nevertheless, principal teachers were typical in elementary schools through the 1950s and into the early 1960s . . . " (Norton, 2013, p. 7). Recommended position descriptions for the assistant school principal are considered in depth in Chapter 3 of the book.

Statement #3 is false. On the contrary, school principals without administrative assistance welcome such support. Excessive workload is named high on the principal's list of factors that inhibit their effectiveness and result in job dissatisfaction. More and more, those persons aspiring to the positions of school principal as a career are giving thought to their work life. The former view of "living to work" is changing toward the concept of "working to live."

Statement #4 is false. In 2014, the median annual salary of assistant school principal approximated $77,962. This figure represents approximately 82 percent of the approximate median salary for school principals of $95,962. Statistics for national salaries are always approximate and differ depending on such factors as the sample population used for the statistical report.

Statement #5 is false. Although the tasks and competencies for assistant school principals do differ depending on school grade levels, school student population, and other such factors, major studies have been completed in this regard. As early as 1987, Norton and Kriekard surveyed assistant principals in a six-state area to determine their real and ideal competencies. Later, in 2008, Norton and Farrar authored a comprehensive work, *Competency-Based Preparation of Educational Administrators*. The publication included seven primary tasks and twenty-six related competencies necessary for effectiveness in the role of the assistant secondary school principal. The major tasks of the assistant principal were as follows:

1. To exercise proper management of the school for unplanned as well as planned daily operations of the school.
2. To perform as a leader of the school in the area of staff personnel.
3. To develop and maintain effective community relations.
4. To function as an instructional leader of the school.
5. To function as the organizer and administrator of student activities and athletics.
6. To function as the school leader for pupil personnel services.
7. To plan and participate in professional growth activities.

The results of a mini-survey questionnaire sent to school principals serving all school levels revealed that assistant principals have many other tasks that require personal competency. These results are presented later in Chapter 2.

Statement #6 is false. "Assistant principals as a group have not been the subject of a substantial number of formal research studies" (Sutter, 1996, pp. 106–113). As Glanz (1994) points out, the research available on the role and responsibilities of the assistant principal is extremely limited. Many other researchers have pointed out that research on the assistant school principal has been sparse (Phillips, 2007; Gaston, 2005; Kaplan & Owings, 1999). According to Celikten (1998), research on the assistant principal as an instructional leader is virtually non-existent. In fact, the role of the assistant principal is considered one of the least researched and least discussed topics in professional journals and books that focus on educational leadership (Weller & Weller, 2002).

Statement #7 is false. As many researchers have noted, the actual tasks and responsibilities of assistant school principals do not serve them well in giving them a sound foundation for entering the position of school principal. As pointed out by Panyako and Rorie as early as 1987, "while the role of the assistant school principal may be appropriate in freeing the principal to do management work, the role fails to fit the modern assistant principal" (p. 7). Although the role of the assistant school principal has changed in many schools since 1987, contemporary changes in educational goals and objectives call for further attention to the leadership roles that assistant school principals can play relative to such functions as student learning, human resources administration, staff professional growth and development and other new issues and new needs.

The topic of role responsibilities of contemporary assistant principals is discussed in several other chapters of the book. For example, Chapter 3 centers on the assistant school principal as a student advocate. Chapter 4 views the work of the assistant school principal as a learning leader.

Statement #8 is false. On the contrary, increasing competitive alternatives for educating students, new mandates from federal, state and local governance bodies, the demands for accountability on the part of educators at all levels of education, and competition for available funds for supporting educational programs have brought about the need for major increases in the positive marketing of local school programs and competing in the political climate that serves to control the policies for local school operations.

No longer can educational leaders accept the precept of "keeping education out of politics." "School board members and superintendents must be keenly aware of the political landscape as they seek to carry out the mission of educating the children of a diverse public. School leaders need to develop frameworks to help them navigate the evolving landscape of educational politics" (Norton et al., 1996, p. 91). School principals and assistant principals must come to understand the complexity of the kind of political powers used to influence decisions about the allocation of resources and policy decisions that affect their school's operations.

Statement #9 is true. This procedure for determining the "daily tasks" of the assistant school principal relates closely to the conditions cited in statement #7 above. The lack of specificity of the assigned job tasks of the assistant school principal remains in evidence today. However, more school districts have developed position descriptions for assistant principals in their schools, even though many tend to be quite general and therefore provide little direction for the assistant principal to give a responsible response to his/her work tasks.

Statement #10 is false. Since more contemporary position descriptions of the assistant school principal indeed are including responsibilities for instructional leadership, the statement is trending toward a "true" answer. However, empirical evidence suggests that managerial duties rather than academic leadership have dominated assistant principals' position assignments. What is needed, however, is specificity in the assistant principal's instructional leadership role. How is the role responsibility to be accomplished? What specific tasks and related competencies are required in the position? In some cases today, especially at the secondary school level, the title of one of the assistant school principals in the school is, "Assistant Principal for Curriculum and Instruction." The topic of the assistant school principal as an instructional leader is discussed later in Chapter 4 of this book.

Distributive Leadership: What Is It and What Are Its Implications for Improving the Role of the Assistant School Principal?

Distributive leadership includes a wide variety of strategies that are designed to meet the goals and objectives of the school by using the leadership knowledge and skills available within the school and the community. In its most common form, the school principal shares leadership responsibilities with one or more assistant principals, department chairs or grade-level supervisors. Other distributive models include the leadership knowledge and skills of teacher-leaders, principal-teachers, co-principals, community support personnel or agencies, teacher-led schools and others.

Models That Represent "New Ways" to Extend Leadership Roles Within Your School

The best distributive leadership model for your school is the one that allows you and other school personnel to spend more time on the improvement of student academic performance by capitalizing on the leadership talent that exists within the school community. In addition, distributive leadership models provide opportunities for a balanced work life for the school principal and also facilitate the retention of quality school leaders.

Perhaps the use of the words "new ways" in the heading of this section is not completely appropriate. In most cases a variety of distributive leadership models already is in practice. For example, schools in Long Beach, California were using a co-principal model as early as 1997. We will consider the co-principal model and other distributive leadership models that may or may not fit your school's organizational needs. However, the illustrative models might suggest other ways in which your school could benefit by creating distributive leadership strategies in your school.

Let's Consider Several Distributive Leadership Models

(1) The Traditional Principal, Assistant Principal Model for Administration

- Conducts conferences with parents, students and teachers concerning student issues with full attention to student rights.
- Supervises student service activities and shares responsibilities with teachers and others in establishing and implementing meaningful student activity programs.

Administration Functions

- Assumes the leadership of the school in the absence of the head principal.
- Assists in carrying out the daily school administrative activities including teaching assignments, substitute teacher assignments, monitoring of student attendance, student transportation, scheduling, and emergency matters that occur.
- Takes an active role in working with the school principal, department heads.

Leadership—This model remains as the most common distributive leadership model in practice. Previously, we have pointed out the disadvantages of this model in earlier sections of this chapter including the fact that the assistant school principal's role too often is not well defined. Nevertheless, effective support given to the school principal by one or more assistant principals, department chairpersons and/or grade-level supervisors serves the school's learning culture mission in several ways. The need for a planned and definitive position description for the assistant principal is imperative. In addition, the role of the assistant principal should tie closely to the administrative functions of the entire school. Completely separating the tasks of the assistant principal and the principal inhibits the use of the strengths of both individuals to lead the school in its primary mission of student learning. In many cases, separation of services does little to implement an accession strategy for moving quality personnel into the principal's role.

In order for the assistant principal to be effective in meeting the role objective of being a learning leader, preparation programs in higher education must improve. In most cases, preparation for school administration centers on the responsibilities of the school principal and tend to neglect the entry position of assistant principal. Core courses commonly center on school facility planning, school finance, school law, organizational management, business management, public relations, and a part-time internship that centers on the work of the school principal, not the logical entry position of assistant principal. It isn't that these offerings are not important in the work of a school principal; however, present and future preparation for positions in educational administration must give much more attention to instructional leadership, curriculum and instruction, human resources administration, talent management, developing healthy school climates, becoming student advocates, administration of the support staff, performance assessment and evaluation, professional growth and development, student personnel practices, accountability assessments, school–community relations and building a learning culture in the school.

Figure 1.1 is an example of the traditional model of school administration. The model suits a large high school with a student enrollment of 1,500 to 2,500 students. The assistant principal assignments are typical, but other role assignments would be appropriate depending on the program emphasis and needs of the particular high school.

Although the development of position analysis and position descriptions for the assistant principal's role will be discussed additionally later in this book, Box 1.1 sets forth an example of a common position description for an assistant school principal in a high school. Note that the position description sets forth the specific responsibilities for several important school functions with emphasis placed on responsibilities for learning leadership.

Board of Education

Wymore Community High School

School Principal - - - - - Site-Based Council

Assistant Principal for Pupil Personnel Services (Registrar)	Assistant Principal for Curriculum & Instruction	Assistant Principal for Human Resources Administration	Assistant Principal for Athletics and School Activities
Guidance	Curriculum Development	Recruitment	Sports Management
Testing	Performance Assessment	Selection	Intramural Activities
Discipline	Supervision	Orientation	Activity Scheduling
Safety & Welfare	Performance Evaluation	Assignment	Campus Environment
Health Services	Special Needs Program	Performance Assessment	Transportation
Cafeteria Services	Gifted Student Program	Growth & Development	Health Activities
School Climate	School Climate	School Climate	School Climate
		Support Staff	Coaches, Asst. Coaches
	Academic Department Chairs	Personnel Accounting	Accounting/Budgeting

Students

FIGURE 1.1 Example of a Large High School Traditional Administration Model

Box 1.1 Position Description—Assistant Principal (High School)

Assistant Principal—High School

Employer:	Wymore School District
Administrative Position:	Assistant Principal
School Site:	Wymore South High School
Salary:	Administrator Salary Schedule

Position Description

The assistant principal reports to the school principal

Major Position Responsibilities

Instructional Leadership

1. Participates in the planning, development, implementation and assessment of the school's curricular and extra-curricular and educational programs.
2. Serves as an instructional leader by collecting appropriate data relative to student academic performance and works with the teaching faculty to evaluate student academic achievement results.
3. Assists in the implementation of federal, state and local school board achievement standards by participating in training sessions, classroom observations, and collecting and analyzing student achievement data for the purposes of identifying program strengths and areas where improvement is needed.
4. Participates in the identification of professional growth needs and the implementation of specific individual and group activities that lead to individual and group improvements.
5. Assists the school principal in the assessment and evaluation of certificated and classified members of the staff.
6. Recommends funding in the school's budget for the instructional equipment and materials needed to meet the goals and objectives of the school's instructional programs.

Human Resources Administration

1. Participates directly in planning and implementing the human resources processes of selecting, assigning, orienting, evaluating, and developing faculty and support personnel.
2. Conducts employee performance assessments and evaluations. Implements follow-up personnel conferences relative to evaluation results. Confers with employees relative to the development and implementation of a plan for professional growth and development.

Fostering a Positive School Climate

1. Uses valid instruments for measuring the work climate that exists in the school. Fosters a positive school climate by providing opportunities for active learning, individualizing performance expectations, providing opportunities for involvement in decision making and working to provide necessary instructional resources.

Student Personnel Services

1. Participates in the collaborative processes that result in a safe school environment. Ensures the development of necessary school rules and administers

student discipline and teachers in compiling budgetary information and determining expenditure priorities.

2. Assumes responsibility for the coordination of special school services and programs related to support personnel, student transportation, cafeteria services, health services and extra-curricular activities

3. Implements the laws, policies and administrative regulations set forth by federal, state, local school board and local school agencies and offices.

4. Implements time management strategies that permit a more productive use of administrative time and places first priorities at the top of the work-to-do list.

School Public Relations and Marketing Responsibilities

1. Sets forth an effective plan for involving the school-community in the development of a guiding school mission that centers on establishing a learning culture in the school.

2. Uses effective methods to scan internal and external environments of the school for the purposes of knowing the school and community educational needs and initiating programs and activities that support the accomplishment of these needs.

Supervisory Responsibilities

1. Works with the school principal in the supervision of the professional and classified staffs of the school as assigned by the school principal. Assumes major roles in administering the human resources processes for the school, the performance evaluation of the faculty and support staff and providing mentoring and professional growth programs with individual employees.

Working conditions

The position necessitates irregular working hours including frequent evening and weekend responsibilities for student, parent and professional activities. The position demands the ability to work cooperatively with a wide variety of clientele and community agencies. Both oral and written competencies are required on a daily basis.

Stress situations encountered call for the ability to maintain self-control at all times. Emergency situations necessitate the ability to act wisely under pressure. The assistant principal must be able to work competently on several tasks and meet target dates within specific periods of time.

We emphasize the concept of competency-based leadership because of its potential for providing the knowledge, skills and personal characteristics of paramount importance for effective performance by the assistant school principal. Competency-based leadership, however, is much more than the implementation of standards or technical skill in leadership performance. As will be illustrated by the tasks, competencies and related indicators of competencies presented throughout the chapters of the book, the importance of character, trust, passion and purpose must be foremost in the leader's behaviors. The school's purposes, vision, values and commitment must also be competently demonstrated.

2) The Co-Principal Model for Administrative Leadership

The **co-principal model** commonly divides the organizational functions between two individuals; one who specializes in the area of curriculum and instruction and one who specializes in organizational management. In the first case, the school co-principal is able to spend more time in building a learning culture in the school and attending to student achievement. The second co-principal focuses on management functions relating to personnel, school facilities, budget matters, and registrar matters. Supervision of the classified personnel, school safety, and student transportation is also the responsibility of this co-principal.

Co-principals by definition are given the authority to administer the position tasks as assigned. Although the school principal remains as the final authority in school business matters, the co-principal is assigned as the administrative leader for each job task. Common examples of co-principals include: co-principal of instruction, co-principal of student safety and welfare, co-principal of athletic/sport activities, co-principal of faculty/staff personnel, co-principal of administrative services, co-principal of support personnel, and co-principal of special programs. In the case of only one co-principal assigned to the school, the title of co-principal is sufficient.

Job analyses and job descriptions of the co-principal(s) are specific in directing work assignments and responsibilities. In some cases, the co-principal might be given the title of co-principal of student personnel, co-principal of human resources administration or other titles that fit the case. Although co-principals work closely with the school principal and other co-principals in the school, administrative programs, problems and procedures are channeled through the co-principal's office. Personnel hiring, orientation, assignment, performance evaluation, professional growth and development, for example, are channeled through the office of the co-principal for personnel services, although co-principals for other school functions are cooperatively involved in decisions that relate to their areas of expertise. Note that we use the terms "job" and "position" description interchangeably throughout the text.

Co-principals report to the school principal. The school principal administers the performance evaluations of co-principals. On school matters that are adequately defined by the co-director's job description, school district policy, administrative regulation or school rule, the co-administrator is expected to act decisively on a matter without the necessity of always "first checking" with the school principal.

The universal job description statement of ". . . and other tasks as assigned by the school principal" is not appropriate for the job descriptions of co-principals. The official title of the co-principal and the specificity of the job description serve the purpose of directing a task, decision or problem to the proper co-principal. In case of the principal's absence, the case at hand determines which co-principal handles the matter.

The primary goal of the co-principal model is to increase the administrative attention given to the development and implementation of a learning climate in the school. Another important purpose is to share the increasing responsibilities of the principalship and hopefully improve the retention of quality school principals who seek a balance in their personal work life.

(3) The Specialist Assistant Principal Model

The assistant principal specialist organization appears to be an increasing leadership model, especially in larger high schools. In this model, the school principal works with several assistant principals who assume the leadership for such major functions as curriculum and instruction, human resources administration, pupil personnel services, athletics, school marketing, public relations, and school activities. Each specialist reports to the school principal.

The rationale for the specialist model centers on the fact that certain major administration functions increasingly are being delegated to the local school. Human resources administration, for example, has become an increasing responsibility of the local school. School principals have become responsible for hiring, assigning, orienting, evaluating and developing certificated and non-certificated employees in their school.

The specialist model sometimes includes specialists in the community who serve as "enrichment teachers" or "administrator specialists" on a regular or occasional basis.

For example, a business teacher might schedule a local business expert to serve as the enrichment teacher relative to a unit on the use of technology in business practices today. Or, the school principal or assistant principal might utilize a local law firm or accounting firm to work with him or her on the school's budget for the forthcoming school year. Overlooking the use of the expertise that exists in every school community has been one of the shortcomings of educational practice for many years. Although we speak of the school community and school partnership, speaking about them is commonly the last thing we do; implementing them is another thing.

(4) The Teacher Talent Model

Give some thought to the kinds of talent that exists among your teaching faculty in the school. The use of these talents for sharing administrative leadership in the school has great potential for achieving needed support for the school principal, developing administrative talent within the school, providing relevant experience for teachers who aspire to positions in administration, reducing the escalating position responsibilities of the school principal, and improving many of the ongoing administrative functions required in any school.

The following entries suggest area responsibilities whereby employees in your school might participate in the administrative leadership of your school. You will be able to identify how the special talents of your staff might take the leadership for other administrative activities that must be performed. Be fully aware of the present workloads of members of your staff before asking them for additional service. For example, the workload of each secondary school teacher on your staff can be readily measured by the use of such instruments as the Douglass Load Formula (1951) or the Norton/Bria Formula for Measuring Elementary School Teacher Load (1992). These useful instruments are presented later in the chapter.

Selected Examples of Administrative Services by Teacher Personnel

Business teachers—Budgets, purchasing, accounting

Home-economic teachers—Food services, student nutrition information

Vocational/industrial arts teachers—Facility planning, maintenance and plant safety

Speech teachers—Verbal communications, speech preparation, public presentations

Elementary school teachers—Learning leadership, school–community relations

English teachers—Written communications, school information flyers, parent newsletters

Foreign language teachers—Community relations/communications

Social studies teachers—Aspects of school law, student rights, civics

Athletics coaches—Community support, public relations

Fine arts—Public relations, school fine arts activities.

How do you gain the participation of your teachers in such administrative activities? You ask them! You most likely will be surprised at their interest in participating in this regard. School principals have the responsibility of developing **learning-leaders** in their school. Teacher learning-leaders can serve the administration goals and objectives of the school in the following ways (Norton & Kelly, 2013, p. 99):

1. Designing curriculum
2. Coaching and mentoring
3. Serving as a resource teacher
4. Helping teachers reach goals
5. Chairing an improvement team
6. Demonstrating teaching methods
7. Teaching a recommended instructional intervention
8. Observing other teachers on the teacher's request
9. Explaining school achievement data results to stakeholders
10. Serving as data analyzer for grade levels or subject matter areas.

What adjustments can be made to provide time for teachers to serve administratively? Improvements in current practices of any kind require the recognition that some changes will be necessary. As noted by Norton, 2013,

> Although some adjustments would be necessary relative to the teacher's classroom assignment, the benefits to the teacher, school principal, and school program would seem to offset expenses related to the teacher's time away from the classroom. The teacher has the opportunity for valuable administrative experience, part of the school principal's increasing workload is reduced, and certain aspects of the school's program activities are enhanced.
>
> (pp. 152–153)

(5) The Teacher-Led Model

Although there is no one model that illustrates teacher-led schools, it most commonly features a school without a principal where the teaching staff runs the school. Participants of this model are of the opinion that if they are to be held accountable for student achievement results, they should be the decision-makers as to how student learning is to be achieved; only when teachers are the ones who are in charge of determining their own teaching will they truly be considered as professionals. **Teacherpreneurs** is one of the new terms used for innovative teachers who serve as leaders in schools.

Little or no research is available that examines the teacher-led model's contentions with performance results. Many questions facing the teacher-led model remain unanswered. Who answers the myriad questions that are faced on a daily basis by all schools in operation? How are the support personnel hired and supervised? How are the daily administrative tasks of a school completed effectively? If the teachers as a whole are the decision makers relative to curriculum and instruction, student services, hiring teaching and support personnel and student services, when and how are these necessities met and implemented? How is instructional performance assessed and evaluated? Is the process one of "You evaluate me and I will evaluate you"? Or if the teacher is to determine the teaching curriculum and methods, is a self-evaluation sufficient?

Participants and/or promoters of the teacher-led model do have answers to most questions set forth, but hard evidence of the results is not available. The following briefs are those stated by various teacher-led school proponents.

Teacher-Led Proponents' Statements

TLP-1   Teacher-led schools that focus on school improvement can engage the skill and spirit of their staffs better than top-down governance systems.

TLP-2   Teachers can share some of the administrative duties. One of them might work just on administrative duties. It must be made clear that he or she is not a boss.

TLP-3   The teacher-led school is the key to accountability. They can't be held accountable for things over which they have no control.

TLP-4   Teacher job satisfaction has decreased substantially over the last five years. One reason is that they are being held accountable for things over which they have no control.

TLP-5   Fine, hold us accountable, but let us do it our way.

TLP-6   Staff members spend considerable time collaborating and that enables them to arrive at a common understanding of the school's direction and policies. Major issues are resolved by consensus or, on thorny issues, by secret ballot.

TLP-7   Our success is based on widely-accepted core principles, strong commitment by staff, union leadership, time to collaborate, meaningful professional development, student-centered curriculum, exceptional parental support, and a supportive administration (note: school is the only teacher-led school in a large city's school district).

TLP-8   Facilitating the dialogue with the administrative tasks are two lead teachers who are half-time classroom teachers. They also serve as the interface between parents and the school and between the school and the district school department.

TLP-9 While each teacher-led school is unique, the shared decision-making is what defines them. The teachers' participation tends to create a culture quite different from that in a principal-led school: Teachers can't hide behind the classroom door or complain about policies, because they have to come up with the solutions.

TLP-10 So the key that makes a partnership school work is **autonomy**; the ability to budget, select the faculty, and decide the approach to learning that will work best for the students.

Teacher-Led Opponents' Statements

TLO-1 I was employed in a teacher-governed school for one semester. Teachers tell the school principal what to do. How does this work administratively? It doesn't.

TLO-2 In my experience, external counselors were used to observe and then confer with teachers on the acceptable or unacceptable performance. Follow-up improvement activities most often were left hanging.

TLO-3 What one hears about the great success of teacher-led governance schools comes from the teachers of those schools. What would one expect to hear? Objective research on the model is missing and sorely needed.

TLO-4 Teacher workload is an ongoing problem in most schools. How can teachers in teacher-led schools do justice to student learning and meet the administrative tasks that all schools must perform?

TLO-5 I wanted to work part-time and a teacher-led school had such an opening. I felt that I was riding on a runaway train. The teacher-led governance model might appear to be more democratic but it certainly is not results-oriented. When a matter needs a decision it first has to go back to the teachers. The solution just has to wait.

TLO-6 Who is to judge how well the school is doing? Who assesses and evaluates the effectiveness of teacher performance? The teachers themselves?

TLO-7 There are volumes of research that support the fact that the school leadership by the principal is the key to an effective school program. Yet, models such as teacher-led governance expect us to replace the principal with a group of teachers none of which have administrative preparation. That just doesn't make sense. We fully support efforts to use teacher talents in the fostering of improved administrative functions within the school. The effectiveness of teacher-led schools has yet to be determined; much more research relative to student learning outcomes and the ability of such a model to administer a school effectively is imperative. Each of the foregoing distributive leadership models has positive factors that will find their way into improved administrative practices. And, some of the contentions associated with each model will fall through the cracks of the ever-flowing changes that take place in education.

A volume of research has been completed that supports the fact that the leadership of the school principal is the key to an effective school program. When the school principal works collaboratively with other members of the faculty toward the implementation of a learning culture in the school, good things happen in the arena of student academic performance. The research also underscores the immediate need to improve the opportunities for the assistant principal(s) to come of age and contribute in a meaningful way to the school's mission of fostering a learning-centered school. This goal can only be enhanced by improving the preparation of the assistant school principal and assigning role responsibilities to the position that facilitate the implementation of a learning environment in the school. Strategies, programs and recommendations for bringing new life to the position of assistant school principal are presented in each of the following chapters of this book.

Summary

The fact that school principals nationally are facing new administrative responsibilities without a corresponding support system is common knowledge in education today. The calls for meeting student achievement standards determined by federal, state and local agencies have brought about new pressures for accountability relative to improved classroom instruction. Administrative responsibilities increasingly have been delegated to the local school. The inability to hire and retain quality administrators at the school level has brought attention to new administrative models that demand higher quality service from assistant school principals and have given rise to teachers' demands for more autonomy in the classroom and more power relative to curriculum matters and how decisions are to be made in schools.

Both empirical evidence and research have pointed out that preparation for the assistant principal's position has been unsatisfactory; what assistant principals do commonly is determined by the daily assignment of the school principal. When position descriptions are determined for the assistant principal, assigned tasks all too often are not related to the real work of a school principal. Thus, it is of paramount importance that the school principal be aware of the knowledge and competencies required of effective leaders in the position of assistant principal. Emphasis on student discipline and other management tasks tends to leave the assistant principal unprepared for accession to the principal's role.

As a result of the problems facing the position of school principal, fewer assistant principals are aspiring to the role of principal as a career and school principals are questioning their interest in continuing in the role; work–life balance has become a primary concern.

Student academic achievement mandates have placed student learning as the number one responsibility of the school principal. Over the years, the management aspects of educational administration have overridden the attention given to how students learn and how to develop a learning culture in the school.

Mandates set forth by federal, state and local education agencies call for ongoing classroom visits, performance assessments and evaluations, and follow-up plans for instructional improvement. Although performance evaluation processes have improved, assistant school principals in too many instances have not completed programs for meeting quality evaluator requirements.

Student academic performance results, along with the increasing workload of school principals, have brought about the promotion of new ways to distribute administrative leadership in schools. Some models are supported primarily by unions, teachers' associations, or by other teacher groups. Several distributive leadership models were discussed in the chapter. Effective research is needed to determine if the contentions surrounding each one will be confirmed educationally.

The chapter made clear the fact that teacher talent can be used effectively in several ways to serve the goals and objectives of the school's mission administratively. We endorse the involvement of teachers in teacher-led administrative activities, but strongly believe that the leadership role of the school assistant principal and principal will determine the success of contemporary schools.

Discussion Questions

1. Consider the school administration of the school you know best. Which one of the five distributive leadership models discussed in the chapter does your school reflect? What, if any, changes would you make or like to make in the school's administrative operations as presently practiced?

2. When teachers are assigned to leadership activities in the school, their classroom instruction must be attended. Give thought to innovative ways to assure the continuation of quality instruction for students during the

time a teacher is released from the classroom for teacher leadership activities. For example, how might large-group instructional activities be scheduled for students to accommodate the teacher's release?

3. Five models for distributive leadership were discussed in the chapter. Review the discussion for each distributive leadership model discussed in the chapter and then list your opinion as to the two primary benefits of each model. In turn, list two concerns that you believe must be addressed in each model.

4. Consider the preparation that you have experienced relative to the profession of educational administration. How would you assess the quality of experiences that you have had relative to the position of assistant school principal? If you have aspirations for a career in school administration, how would you assess your preparedness for the role of assistant school principal? If you are an assistant principal or principal, to what extent were you prepared to assume these administrative roles?

CASE STUDIES

Case 1.1 Request for an Assistant Principal to Be Added to the Staff

Principal Delgado's elementary school enrollment for next school year is projected to reach 550. By district policy, a school enrollment of 500 is minimum for having an assistant principal. Just having the required minimum number of students does not guarantee that such a position will be approved, rather the need for the position and its position tasks are viewed as selection criteria among the schools competing for the added position each year. A brief memo to the school superintendent stating the need and proposed responsibilities for the new assistant principal is required.

Principal Delgado wanted to check out her thoughts on this matter with her two grade-level supervisors and asked them to meet with her after school. At the meeting, Principal Delgado read the following letter draft to the supervisors.

> To: Dr. Wallace Burnett, Supt.
> From: Alisa Delgado, Principal, Meadow Lark Elementary School
> Re: Request for Assistant Principal
>
> Since Meadow Lark Elementary School will surpass the school enrollment requirement of 500 pupils next year, I am requesting the addition of an assistant school principal. As you certainly are aware, the responsibilities

of school principals in the Washington School District have increased tremendously during the last few years. The federal, state and school board mandates have increased my workload in the areas of curriculum, instruction and student achievement outcomes; performance evaluations for the teaching staff now assume more than one-third of my time. The new testing program will add more work for my office as well.

I would plan to use the new assistant principal in three specific ways. First, we need someone to assume responsibility for handling all student discipline matters. Second, we need help with such management tasks as bus scheduling, attendance monitoring and playground supervision. Having someone to assume these responsibilities would permit me to spend much more time on other management tasks, including the school budget and public relations.

I will be pleased to furnish additional information upon your request.

"Well, what do you think?" asks Principal Delgado.

Question

1. One of the grade-level supervisors, Carlos Perez, is a likely candidate to assume the new role of assistant principal if such a position is approved. Assume the role of Carlos in this case and be first to respond to Principal Delgado's question. What do you think about the contents of the memo and Principal Delgado's citations of anticipated responsibilities for the assistant principal's position? What is your response? How might you best serve Principal Delgado and the Meadow Lark School program?
2. This case might be an opportunity to re-organize the administration of Meadow Lark Elementary School. Suggest a school organization that includes a new employee in the role of assistant principal. How might you visualize such a re-organization?

References

Austin, B.D., & Brown, A.L. (1970). *Report of the assistant principalship of the study of the secondary school principalship.* Reston, VA: National Association of Secondary School Principals.

Celikten, M. (1998). The instructional leadership tasks of high school assistant principals and factors that enhance or inhibit the enactment of their tasks. Unpublished doctoral dissertation, University of Wisconsin–Madison.

Copland, M. (2001). The myth of the superprincipal. *Phi Delta Kappan*, 82, 525–532.

Douglass, H.R. (1951). The 1950 revision of the Douglass high school teaching load formula. *NASSP Bulletin*, 35, 13–34.

Dunleavy, C.S. (2011). *Mobility of assistant principals: Examining their roles, accomplishments, and aspirations.* Ann Arbor, MI: ProQuest Dissertations.

Gaston, D.W. (2005). Defining the roles and responsibilities of public school assistant principals in Virginia. Unpublished dissertation. College of William and Mary, Williamsburg, VA.

Glanz, E. (1994). Redefining the role of the assistant principal. *The Clearing House*, 67(5), 283–287.

Institute for Educational Leadership (October, 2007). *Leadership for student learning: Reinventing the principalship.* Washington, D.C.: Author.

Kaplan, L., & Owings, W. (1999). Assistant principal: The case for shared instructional leadership. The National Association of Secondary School Principals. *The Bulletin*, 83(610), 80–94.

NASSP (2007). *Changing role of middle level and high school leader: Learning from the past—preparing for the future.* Reston, VA: author.

Norton, M.S. (December 2002–January 2003). Let's keep our quality school principals on the job, *The High School Journal*, 86(2), 50–56.

Norton, M.S. (2013). *Competency-based leadership: A guide for high performance in the role of the school principal.* Lanham, MD: Rowman & Littlefield Education.

Norton, M.S., & Bria, R. (1992). Toward an equitable measurement of elementary school teacher load. *Record in Elementary School Administration and Supervision*, 13(1), 62–66.

Norton, M.S., & Farrar, R.D. (1987). *Competency-based administration of educational administrators: Tasks, competencies and indicators of competencies.* College of Education, Tempe. Tempe: Arizona State University Press.

Norton, M.S., & Farrar, R.D. (2008). *Competency-based preparation for educational administrators: Tasks, competencies and indicators of competencies.* Department of Educational Leadership & Policy Studies, College of Education, Tempe, AZ: Arizona State University.

Norton, M.S., & Kelly, L.K. (2013). *The principal as a learning leader: Motivating students by emphasizing achievement.* Lanham, MD: Rowman & Littlefield.

Norton, M.S., & Kriekard, J.A. (1987). Real and ideal competencies for the assistant principal. *NASSP Bulletin*, 71(501), 23–30.

Norton, M.S., Webb, L.D., Dlugosh, L.L., & Sybouts, W. (1996). *The school superintendency: New responsibilities, new leadership.* Needham Heights, MA: Allyn & Bacon.

Panyako, D., & Rorie, L. (October, 1987). Improving the assistant principalship. *NASSP Bulletin*, 71(501), 6–8.

Phillips, D. (2007). Middle school principals' perceptions of the role and function of the assistant principalship. Unpublished doctoral dissertation, University of the Pacific, Stockton, CA.

Pierce, P.R. (1935). *The origin and development of the public school principalship.* Chicago: University of Chicago Press.

Sutter, M.R. (1996). What do we know about the job and career satisfaction of secondary school assistant principals? *NASSP Bulletin*, 80(April), 108–111.

Weller, L.D., & Weller, S.J. (2002). *The assistant principal: Essentials for effective school leadership.* Thousand Oaks, CA: Corwin Press.

Competency-Based Leadership

Improving the Role of Assistant Principal by Focusing on the Knowledge, Skills, and Competencies Required by the Position

---

Primary chapter goal:

To upgrade the position of assistant principal by implementing competency-based administration.

Consider the process of interviewing a candidate for an assistant principal's position. Which of the following questions would most likely give answers that would be most helpful toward making the hiring decision? (1) Where did you do your administrative internship and what administrative experience have you had to date? What is your career goal? or (2) Tell us about a decision that you had to make that you knew would not go well with an individual, school team or group of people. How did you handle the decision-making process and what did you do regarding the negative reactions? Although the answer to question #1 would provide some experience information, it would appear that such information could easily be found on the application form submitted by the candidate. On the other hand, question #2 is quite likely to provide some evidence of the candidate's competency relative to decisiveness, communication, leadership, resilience, conflict management and other competencies. This chapter centers on improving the position of assistant school principal by focusing on competency-based strategies for upgrading the leadership responsibilities of the role.

Why Competency-Based Leadership?

In Chapter 1, various authorities pointed out the historical problems of a nebulous assistant principalship. That is, the position has lacked direction, authority, and accountability. Competency-based leadership can help improve these conditions in a school by:

- Defining specifically the kind(s) of knowledge and skills needed to accomplish the school's mission and indicating how they are demonstrated in the performance of the assistant principal.

- Establishing a framework of knowledge and skills needed to perform the required tasks of the assistant principal's position.

- Linking the required position competencies of the assistant principal to the school's mission, goals and objectives.

- Using the position competencies to identify the individual growth and development needs of the assistant principal.

- Establishing purposes related to performance assessment and evaluation requirements; clarifying what performance is expected of the assistant school principal.

- Encouraging the creativity of the practicing assistant principal. Knowing what is to be done in the position opens the door for personal initiative in getting the job done.

- Fostering efficiency in performance by defining the tasks of the assistant principal's position and indicating how the tasks can best be achieved and how such achievements are evidenced in the assistant principal's performance.

- Defining the tasks, competencies and indicators of competencies so that administrative performance of the assistant principal can be assessed, evaluated and improved.

- Giving more objectivity to hiring of assistant principals. Interview procedures can be focused on the knowledge, skills and the candidate's individual abilities as opposed to subjective judgments that are not directly related to position effectiveness.

- Providing a meaningful relationship between the work of the school principal and the assistant principal. Position responsibilities indicate a division of labor and also reveal the evidence of a cooperative, supportive relationship.

The following sections of the chapter will center on defining competency-based leadership and illustrating how the concept can be applied to the position of assistant principal in practice. In doing so, two important objectives will be to define the position of assistant principal in terms of competency-based leadership and to present examples whereby competency-based leadership is beneficial in developing and implementing effective programs and activities relating to personnel hiring, professional development, performance evaluation, accountability and other relevant administrative functions.

Tasks, Competencies and Indicators of Competencies

When you enter the practice of school administration, you cannot escape being given important administrative responsibilities that require knowledge and skills for accomplishing the responsibilities successfully. We refer to these major responsibilities as **tasks**. In regard to role success, we refer to the abilities that you need to fulfill the tasks successfully as **competencies**. The behaviors that you implement and the outcomes of the competencies utilized are referred to as **indicators of competencies**. The term **competency** evolves from the Latin roots of the prefix *com* meaning together and the suffix *petere* meaning "to strive at." Thus, competency is viewed as working together or striving for a common goal. Related synonyms include such words as capable, competent, sound and come together. Here is how others have defined the term competency: "Any skills, knowledge, values attitudes, personal attributes or distinguishing qualities and motives (or intent) as demonstrated through behavior which contribute to successful performance of work" (Interdepartmental Committee on Competency-Based Management, Government of Canada, December 13–15, 2006, p. 1) and "Any underlying characteristic of an employee which results in effective and/or superior performance in a job" (Boyatzis, 2009, conceptual paper). Both of the foregoing definitions underscore the qualities of knowledge, skills and attributes of an individual that are demonstrated in successful work performance.

Various tasks and responsibilities of leaders in business and industry were identified in various studies in the early 1960s. As stated by the Hay Group (1996), "Competencies are increasingly what make the world go 'round . . . competencies are being used to guide staffing, training and development, performance management, and compensation practices" (p. 15). During the next forty years, the concept found its way into educational practices. For example, a competency related to the assistant principal serving as the organizer and administrator of the school activities and athletic programs would be the "Ability to plan facility usage and maintain a master activity schedule." Another required competency might be the "Ability to manage fund accounts for student activities and athletics." Later, in Chapter 6, a comprehensive compendium of relevant tasks, competencies and indicators of competencies for the assistant principal is detailed.

Indicators of competencies are those overt behaviors, products and related process outcomes that illustrate one's ability to accomplish the required competencies that define the task. Once again, using the foregoing task and competency of the assistant principal relative to organizing and administering the school activities and athletics, two examples of indicators of competency would include, "Knows and implements the legal aspects of student activity financial accounts" and "Keeps accurate financial records of student activities and athletics."

Implementing the Competency Concept to Upgrade the Assistant Principal's Position

"Every organization will have its own 'competency model' that includes the critical behaviors necessary for success in that culture" (ThinkWise, Inc., 2007, p. 1). Such a model in education commonly defines a set of competencies that center on instructional leadership, pupil personnel services, school climate, instructional performance, personnel administration and other major tasks related to education and administration in school settings.

The significance of a competency-based approach is vested in its application benefits. ThinkWise, Inc. (2007) identifies several possible applications that could benefit your school operations. Such applications include structured interviewing, assessment surveys for identifying future leaders, succession planning, talent mapping, training and development programs, team development, performance evaluation, and others. Attempts to improve the role of the assistant school principal would be expedited by implementing such applications in practice. Both the accomplishment of the school's goals and objectives and the improvement of the performance of the assistant principal could benefit.

Norton (2013) points out the differences between a competency-based school administrator and one who is not. First of all, the competency-based administrator possesses a thorough knowledge of the tasks, competencies and indicators of competencies required in the various administrative roles that he or she supervises. Second, the competency-based administrator understands that the requirements of any school position face ongoing change; tasks and related competencies demand continuous personal growth and development. Third, competency-based administrators know their personal strengths and weaknesses and work from the perspective of their strengths. As noted by Clifton and Nelson (1992), an individual's production quality and quantity are increased significantly when strengths are exercised rather than placing the lion's share of time on trying to overcome one's weaknesses.

Real and Ideal Competencies and Implications for Practice

Norton and Kriekard (1987) surveyed assistant principals in a six-state area relative to those competencies actually performed (**real competencies**) by public school assistant principals and those that should be performed (**ideal competencies**) in order for them to be effective. The study results carry important implications for practice. For example, the study participants viewed every real competency as being below the level that would make the position more effective. For example, on a scale of .001 to 1.000, the competency, "Initiates activities to improve instruction," the real mean rating was .622. The competency's ideal rating was .866. The ideal rating for the competency, "Constantly works to equalize educational opportunities for all students," received a real mean rating of .660; its ideal rating was .905.

The 263 assistant principals validated 59 competencies on the real scale and 91 competencies on the ideal scale. That is, 59 of the real competencies were validated as ones that should be included in a list of assistant principal competencies. Ninety-one of the ideal competencies were validated as ones that should be included. It is obvious that merely learning on the job falls short of what is needed to gain quality within the assistant principal's position. The results also suggest that the assistant principals viewed their role as lacking many of the competencies that were necessary for their position's effectiveness.

Contemporary Competencies as Viewed by Assistant Principals

Competency-based administration can serve to structure the administrative role of assistant principal, increase the authority within the position, provide substance in the work assignments, provide a more sophisticated performance evaluation for the assistant principal and increase the position's relationship to the primary tasks of the school. These goals underscore the primary theme of this book.

A mini-study of the primary tasks/responsibilities of assistant principals was completed by Norton in 2014. A brief questionnaire was competed by each study participant, who was asked to rate the importance of several major position tasks of the assistant principal. Elementary, middle and secondary school assistant principals participated in the study. Each participant was asked to rate the importance of the task entries for the position of assistant school principal in schools today. The results of the study are presented in Table 2.1.

Nine entries were presented for the participant's responses. The rating legend for judging the entries was as follows: 1—low importance; 2—some importance; 3—high importance–highest in importance. One open-ended entry asked participants to list other important responsibilities that should be listed in the role of assistant principal. In the majority of cases, the participant's open-ended entries were such that each could be included under one of the nine major responsibility entries of the questionnaire. Open-ended entries were not given a rating.

TABLE 2.1 Most Important Position Tasks of the Assistant Principal: Mini-Study of Elementary, Middle and Secondary Assistant Principals

Important Assistant Principal Administrative Responsibilities	Mean Statistic
Role as an instructional leader	3.00
Role in student personnel activities including discipline, welfare and safety	3.00
Role in the teacher performance measurement and evaluation	3.00
Role in assessing and maintaining a positive school environment/climate	2.75
Role in working in school public relations with parents and community members	2.75
Role in supervision and evaluation of the school's classified/support staff	2.75
Role in personnel function including hiring, orientation, placement, etc.	2.50
Role in implementing special activities including clubs, sports, etc.	2.50
Role in management activities including budgeting, scheduling, busing, time management and others	2.25

Other Open-Ended Entries (Not rated)

Supervision of interns

Student achievement testing

Development of curricular and extra-curricular programs

Supervises the development of professional development plans for teachers

Takes the leadership for school marketing strategies

Supervision of student services

Assumes role of principal in his/her absence

Three of the nine major tasks derived from the foregoing study are used in Box 2.1 to illustrate an application of the competency-based concept for developing a position description for an assistant school principal. As previously noted, a more detailed discussion of position analyses and position descriptions is presented in Chapter 3.

Box 2.1 An Example of a Partial Position Description for the Assistant Principal Using a Competency-Based Format

Assistant Principal

Employer:	Columbus School District
Administrative Position:	Assistant Principal
School Site:	Columbus South High School
Salary:	Administrative Performance Salary Schedule

Position Description

The assistant principal reports to the school principal

Major Position Tasks

Role as an Instructional Leader

Task 1.0: To function as an instructional leader of the school.

Required Competencies

1.1 Ability to establish a learning culture in the school that focuses on student achievement as the primary purpose of the school.

1.2 Ability to understand how students learn and communicate this knowledge to teachers on the faculty.

1.3 Ability to assess classroom teaching and student achievement data relative to student achievement progress for individual students and the effectiveness of the school's curricular programs.

1.4 Ability to apply knowledge of state standards and district and school goals and achievement targets academically.

1.5 Ability to analyze, interpret and communicate achievement data to faculty personnel for the purposes of identifying program strengths and areas in need of improvement.

1.6 Ability to participate meaningfully in the processes of internal and external scanning relative to the school-community's program needs.

1.7 Ability to communicate achievement data reports to the school principal and staff in a clear and constructive manner.

1.8 Ability to develop a working knowledge of special education curricula including the district gifted and talented program.

1.9 Ability to stand responsible for student achievement results and establish positive attitudes among all faculty personnel for meeting accountabilities in regard to student achievement.

Pupil Personnel Services

Task 2.0: To Function as a Leader for Student Personnel Services

Required Competencies

2.1 Ability to supervise the attendance operation from implementing school board policy to computation of average daily student membership.

2.2 Ability to develop student attendance procedures that conform to state and district policy.

2.3 Ability to implement the legal aspects of state and district attendance policies.

2.4 Ability to supervise and/or develop computerized services for monitoring student attendance.

2.5 Ability to establish effective communication with teachers and parents regarding the status of excessive student absenteeism.

2.6 Ability to implement an effective program for reducing student tardiness and absenteeism through cooperative actions with the students, parents and teachers.

2.7 Ability to provide for effective guidance and counseling services for students.

Task 3.0 To Lead in the Promotion of Positive Community-School Relations and Assume the Leadership for School Marketing Activities.

Role in Fostering a Positive School Climate in the School Required Competencies

3.1 Ability to be knowledgeable of the research relating to school climate and understand its significance in meeting the school's goals and objectives.

3.2 Ability to implement valid assessments of the school's climate and use assessment results to plan improvements as needed.

3.3 Ability to communicate the importance of school climate to all members of the professional and support staff personnel.

3.4 Ability to complete internal and external scanning strategies for the purposes of understanding the strengths and needs of both the school and the school-community.

3.5 Ability to understand the factors that determine a positive school climate and the target areas for implementing improvement.

3.6 Ability to work with the school faculty and staff to develop a set of shared goals to guide the school's programs.

3.7 Ability to provide opportunities for personal growth and development on the part of all school personnel.

3.8 Ability to foster a problem-solving capacity in the school for the purpose of creating an open climate in the school.

3.9 Ability to participate in the development of effective faculty personnel regulations for the school.

Each of the competency entries in Box 2.1 would be followed with appropriate indicators of the competency that serve to demonstrate the overt behaviors and activities that would indicate evidence of successful implementation of the competency. The indicators of competency are not included in the position description of the assistant principal; rather, indicators of competencies are utilized in designing the performance evaluation instrument and determining the individualized professional growth plan. For example, consider the various indicators of competency in Box 2.1. Three such indicators of competency might be: (1) Establishes a meaningful process for the orientation of new faculty and staff personnel, (2) Works cooperatively with teachers in the development of individual improvement plan in accord with the results of performance assessments, and (3) Uses competency-based strategy for assessing the qualities of candidates for teaching positions in the school.

How Competency-Based Methods Can Greatly Improve the Hiring Process

Candidates for teaching positions in schools commonly are asked the question, "Tell us about your teaching experiences. What you have learned from those experiences." "Competency-based interviewing places the emphasis on the applicant's individual ability to relate learning from experience to the position in question" (Experis, 2014, p. 2). When an individual is selected for a position as assistant principal, remember that he or she does not automatically become a qualified interviewer for teaching positions. What does it take to be a competent interviewer? Best fit implies that you have a position in mind that requires certain tasks of responsibility and specific competencies on the part of the position holder. A competency-based position description includes those competencies that are considered essential for success in the position. As interviewer, you need to develop a list of questions to ask the interviewee that reveals how he or she has demonstrated the required competencies.

It is easy to stray from the purpose of the interview, so you need to have back-up questions ready to bring the interview back on target. For example, assume that your leading question was "What do you believe are the traits of a good teacher?" If the candidate strays from a specific response, you might follow with questions such as, "What specific traits have you found to be most effective in promoting student learning in the classroom?" or "How do you deal with individual learning differences among students in the classroom?"

When an interview is scheduled, it is assumed that the candidate has a genuine interest in the position and that you have a genuine interest in the candidate. You will set the stage for your preparation by having a competency-based position description on hand. A successful job–candidate fit is contingent on having a guiding competency model for accurately assessing the fit between the candidate and the position. You should already know the competencies that are needed for realizing success in the position opening. If not, just what would you be looking for? Your job is to learn if the candidate has the abilities to do the tasks of the position successfully. The hiring of a misfit for a position, thinking that she or he can learn on the job, will always be a costly failure.

When determining the competencies that serve to build your list of questions for an interview, it is a good idea to know something of the research on the topic of competencies and success. For example, the two competencies of achievement and impact and influence were identified by Spencer and Spencer (1993) as being critical to high levels of success in most demanding leader positions. **Achievement** is viewed as the behaviors of establishing challenging goals and striving for high performance levels. If the task was to establish challenging goals and high performance, indicators of competencies would be revealed in the leader's actions of setting priorities that led to the desired performance outcomes, using actions that served goal accomplishment and using available faculty talents and resources to meet the desired ends. The competency of **impact and influence** is revealed in the overt actions of the assistant principal that influence the behavior of others in the way that they think and perceive a change in program procedures.

Assume that your school has been giving priority to the matter of school climate and how the climate can be improved (see page 61). You might ask the question, "Tell me about a time when you were involved in a problem relating to job satisfaction in the school. What was the situation? What problems did you face in that situation? What decision had to be made on your part? What were the results of your decision?" Then, take notes regarding the candidate's competencies relating to the skills of achievement, impact and influence, communication, interpersonal relations, problem solving, leadership, teamwork, stress management and decision-making. Use your competency grid to note the fact that the competency was spotted or not spotted in the candidate's response.

Some brief rating scale should be determined in advance. For example, a scale of 5 to 0 (high to low) might be used to rank the quality of the competency as it is illustrated during the interview. The score of zero indicates that the expected competency was not evidenced in the candidate's response.

Tips for Securing Candidate Information That the Position Requires

One problem concerning personnel recruiting has been the use of the same position application for every position opening. The school and school district can enhance the attraction of qualified applicants in several ways. For example, contemporary technology makes possible the easy use of different formats for position applications. Positions differ and so should position applications. Position requirements for a kindergarten teacher differ from those of a sixth-grade teacher. Similarly, position requirements for a social studies teacher differ from those of a foreign language teacher. The applications for these positions should differ, as well as the resumes that would be received.

The use of a competency-based position application encourages the receipt of qualified applicants. The key competency words used in the application for a particular position and the applicant's responses expedite the screening process and the development of a short list of position candidates. Your career aspirations, of course, are of interest to an applicant, but most likely not so much for the school's position needs. Encourage applicants to include a brief statement at the outset of the resume that summarizes his or her qualifications for the position at hand. You want to know just how the applicant can contribute to your school's needs and the position in question.

You will want to know about the applicant's success. If the applicant is new to the teaching profession, recommendations from the individual(s) that supervised their internship are relevant. For those applicants with teaching experience, previous supervisors will be able to provide the best evidence of their success potential. A personal call to these references is most likely to provide the most objective information. In regard to written recommendation, as one principal said, "Darn the person who cannot read between the lines."

Competency-Based Snapshot 2.1: The Interview

Assistant Principal Jarrow was heading to the school's conference room to meet Ron Morris, candidate for the mathematics teacher's position at Wymore East Middle School. As Ms. Jarrow entered the room she was met by Principal Perez and the position candidate.

"Of course, you are Ron Morris. Welcome to Wymore East," said Ms. Jarrow.

"Let's take a seat and get our visit underway."

Principal Perez shook the hand of the candidate and said, "I'll likely see you again later," and then left the room.

"Well," said Ms. Jarrow, "I feel that I know a great deal about you. Your application and cover letter were informative. I hope that the school information sent to you in the mail was helpful to you as well. Your three years as a math teacher in the Whittier School district appeared to be a good learning experience for you. As indicated in the materials, our school staff has been working diligently to create a learning culture in the school toward the goal of realizing academic improvement on the part of each individual in the school. So, my first questions for you are, 'What strengths do you bring to a team?' and 'Tell me about a time when you used these strengths to help a team resolve a problem it was facing.'"

Ron Morris thought for just a moment and then responded. "I think leadership and adaptability are among the strengths that I have been able to use positively during teamwork sessions. Our math curriculum team spent the first of our meetings getting acquainted without really knowing or discussing our task. Before our second meeting, I drafted a purpose/priority questionnaire that focused on what the members viewed as our primary goals and objectives. Several goals were listed for their consideration but a space was available for them to suggest others as well. At the next meeting, the team members' responses were tallied and the top three priorities were determined. We were well on our way to a successful curriculum study."

"Toward the end of the first semester of my second year of teaching, the school board approved a major change in the way teachers were to deal with students with special needs," continued candidate Morris. "The change did not go well with the majority of the teachers. There was even some talk of having the teachers' association take action on the matter. The policy centered on students with special needs being included in the regular classrooms. Both teachers and parents of regular classroom students were up in arms on the matter. At the appropriate time, I stood and made the plea to accept the program change. I pleaded that we were student advocates for all learners and that we really did not know that the concept of inclusiveness would be detrimental to our regular students. In any case, every student had the right to be in the least restricted environment for learning and that we, as professionals, should be the first to accept the possibility of this provision for improved learning for our students."

"I think that my adaptability also was accepted as being professional by other teachers on the staff. After the first year, most problems encountered in the change were faced and resolved. Inclusiveness was a given in our school system."

Take just a few minutes to point out the competencies demonstrated by Ron Morris in his response. What other competencies besides leadership and adaptability might you find in Morris' response? Three additional competency outcomes might include, oral communication, decisiveness, influencing, and risk taking. Other competency-based questions, of course, commonly would be asked in the interview. Why have we taken considerable time to apply the competency-based concept to the teacher selection process? First and foremost is because teacher selection is near the top of the list of the most important tasks that you will perform in the position of assistant principal. In later chapters, the competency-based concept will be illustrated in relation to personnel growth and development and the assistant principal as an instructional leader.

A Lightbulb Experience!

The South Ward School District was informed that its state financial support the following school year would be reduced by 1.3 million dollars. Part of the reduction was due to an expected loss of student enrollment. Another stated reason centered on the state's economic status and reduction of tax income.

As the South Ward school board reviewed the situation it was apparent that budget cuts for the following year must be made. A representative committee consisting of the school superintendent, school principals, teachers, representatives of the parent–teacher association and other parents was appointed to examine the matter and recommend ways for reducing operating costs. After considerable discussion and debate, the committee reported its four recommendations. Just how the recommendations might be considered was left to the school board. By a 7 to 5 vote, the following four recommendations were presented to the school board for consideration: (a) keep all faculty and support staff salaries frozen in place for at least one year; (b) reduce the kindergarten day to one-half time; (c) substantially cut the district and school support staff by one-third; and (d) reduce the administrative staff at the local school level.

The school district's plan for administrator reduction called for the re-assignment to teaching positions of all assistant principals at the elementary school level. Assistant principals at the middle and secondary school levels were requested to submit a brief statement to the board that explained their administrative role in the school and to substantiate its importance in meeting the mission of the school and school district. No further instructions were provided.

After conferring with the school principal on the matter the assistant principal, Manuel Garz, sent the following information to the school board.

> To: Ross Meierhenry, President
> South Ward School District
> From: Manuel Garz, Assistant Principal
> Whittier Middle School
> RE: My Role as Assistant Principal

I have served as school assistant principal at Whittier Middle School for three years. My responsibilities as assistant principal have been exactly that; serving the school principal. That is, I pick up on what the school principal wants me to do for her each day. Some duties seem to be ongoing and some come as surprises each day.

For example, today I met the buses as the students arrived at the school and monitored the campus area where kids tend to gather just before the school opens for classes. Teachers send me their tardy and absence reports during the first class period and I check these over and place the data on the daily attendance register. When time permits, I do follow-up calls to parents regarding student absences.

Hardly a day goes by when I don't have to deal with a student problem. Although I stress to teachers that they should take care of their own classroom discipline, they find it easier just to send the student to me. I follow the school regulations on student discipline to the letter and all students are treated alike (fairness).

The real value of my work comes with taking over the activities that the school principal does not have time to do. On the infrequent days when she is away for business reasons, I do my best to "hold down the fort" until she returns. If this position was eliminated, the principal or someone else would have to do it.

Thank you and I hope to have the opportunity to work with you next year.

The light goes out! Although the foregoing scenario uses fictitious names and is somewhat loosely connected to a factual case, the actual assistant principal was not re-appointed to the administrative role. The letter sent by Manuel Garz underscores the assistant principal's role as one without substance. The letter sent by Manuel lacks evidence of essential position responsibilities related to instructional leadership. No meaningful competencies appear to be required in the position. When the assistant principal's position was disestablished, life in the school went on as usual.

What if an assistant principal in the same school district had sent an abbreviated listing of his position description and it had included a competency-based listing of tasks and responsibilities that emphasized instructional leadership and indicators of successful performance toward achieving the school's and school district's primary mission? In addition, hard data relating to position outcomes would have been impressive as well. If done, one can assume that a "light" would go on brightly within the minds of school board members.

Competency-Based Student Discipline: Are You Kidding Me?

Our purposes in this chapter have centered on illustrating how competency-based practices can enhance the importance of the role of assistant principal for the school's mission of improved student achievement. One of the historical responsibilities of the assistant principal has been in the area of student discipline. The following section serves to illustrate how competency-based methods in discipline procedures can serve to keep students in school and serve as a learning procedure as opposed to strictly a punitive one.

The etymology of the word discipline is interpreted in various languages in a variety of ways. The Latin derivations of the word *disciplina* and *discere* are appropriate for our purposes. *Disciplina* in Latin means instruction and *discere* means to learn. We support the concept of positive school discipline as being most beneficial for students. According to the Los Angeles Unified School District (Fact Sheet), positive behavior intervention methods can improve school climate, improve learning, and reduce disciplinary problems.

Attempts to correct discipline problems by using punitive measures do not serve to improve negative behavior. In addition, zero tolerance methods have negative effects on learning (Skiba et al., 2006). Instead of focusing on the use of punitive discipline methods, positive school discipline places emphasis on dealing with discipline as a teaching and learning opportunity. It is not our purpose here to detail the concept of positive school discipline; rather we want to demonstrate how a competency-based approach for the assistant school principal can be beneficial in disciplinary actions. A selected listing of tasks, competencies and indicators of competencies for the assistant principal's position description relating to discipline is illustrated in Table 2.2.

TABLE 2.2 Competency-Based Application for Student Discipline

Task	Competencies	Indicators of Competency
1.0 To function as the school leader for student personnel services	1.1 Ability to plan and organize procedures for administering student discipline	1.1.1 Selects appropriate disciplinary procedures for individual students that center on positive learning outcomes
		1.1.2 Learns what the research says about the results of various discipline practices.
		1.1.3 Maintains accurate records of discipline cases and follows up results of student learning (i.e., behavior improvements).
		1.1.4 Initiates preventative measures and activities that serve to prevent discipline problems and keep students in the learning environment.

Task	Competencies	Indicators of Competency
		1.1.5 Updates the school's student handbook relative to student discipline and leads information sessions on the topic with students new to the school.
	1.2 Ability to implement climate assessments and evaluate their results	1.2.1 Is knowledgeable of school climate instruments appropriate for teachers, students and parents. Uses resulting data to recommend steps to improve the climate.
	1.3 Ability to understand the importance of a positive school climate for student attitudes and behavior	1.3.1 Studies the research on school climate and provides in-service training for the school's personnel on climate and student attitudes and behavior
		1.3.2 Works with students toward setting and achieving academic goals and personal values.
		1.3.3 Identifies students' personal interests and strengths and uses this information for renewing their focus on learning.
		1.3.4 Implements positive interventions such as peer justice systems, personal counseling, conflict resolution and second-chance modeling.
		1.3.5 Finds ways to recognize and reward positive student behavior.
	1.4 Ability to serve as the school's representative in student discipline hearings	1.4.1 Uses the state laws and school policies for organizing student discipline hearings.
		1.4.2 Shows evidence of fairness in assuring due process for students in administering discipline cases.

Compendium of School Discipline Laws and Regulations for the Fifty States, Washington D.C., and Puerto Rico

We highly recommend that school assistant principals and principals secure a copy of Darling-Churchill et al. (2013), a seminal work on safe supportive learning. This compendium is invaluable for assessing information relative to discipline policy in the various states. Since serious discipline matters such as student suspension are regulated in almost all instances by state law and/or school board policy, knowledge of the contents commonly included in discipline policy would be especially helpful to you.

TABLE 2.3 Discipline Category of In-School Discipline

Specific Sub Categories	Definition
Use of multi–tiered discipline approaches	Directs schools to adopt discipline policies that include graduated consequences and supports.
Teacher authority to remove students from classrooms	Authorizes teachers to remove disruptive students from classrooms, establishes grounds for removal, and may include time limits, parental notification requirements, and procedures for student's return to classrooms.
Alternatives to suspension	Encourages schools to use alternative forms of discipline as a preference over student removal. May include mention of specific alternatives including detention, counseling, or mediation.
Use of corporal punishment	Prohibits the use of corporal punishment or defines the parameters within which corporal punishment is allowed.
Use of student and locker searches	Allows for inspections of students or their personal property while on school grounds, including drug testing, as well as protocols for locker searches.
Other in-school disciplinary approaches	All other statutes and regulations related to in-school disciplinary approaches that do not fit into one of the established categories, such as deferring grades, or withholding grades.

Source: Darling-Churchill, K., Stuart-Cassel, V., Ryberg, R., Schmitz, H., Balch, J., Bezinque, A., and Conway-Turner, J. (2013). *Condominium of School Discipline Laws and Regulations for the 50 States, Washington, D.C. and Puerto Rico*. National Center on Safe Supportive Learning Environments. Available at: http://safesupportive learning.ed.gov/School-Discipline-Compendium.

One section of the school disciplinary compendium mentioned above sets forth a list of categories and definitions of school discipline laws and regulations (see Table 2.3). The four major discipline categories center on (1) general provisions, (2) in-school discipline, (3) out-of-school and exclusionary discipline, and (4) disciplinary approaches addressing specific infractions and conditions. Table 2.3 contains an excerpt related to the second category, in-school discipline. The excerpt provides a brief summary of the contents included in the published compendium. Give special attention to the entries regarding the use of multi–tiered discipline approaches and alternatives to suspension. These category definitions reveal the utilization of positive school discipline.

Empirical evidence has illustrated that competency-based administration can be taught and learned successfully. Formal training programs sponsored by the state's administrators' association or institutions of higher learning have proven effective for competency-based training. Coaching and mentoring, performance evaluation feedback sessions, and the implementation of pilot programs based on competency-based methods are other training methods.

A Post-Quiz Check-Up

Directions: Take two minutes to find the *one* statement below that is not true.

1. An indicator of competencies is an overt behavior, a product or related process that illustrates one's ability to accomplish successfully a required competency of a task.

2. To function as an instructional leader of a school represents a task of an assistant school principal.

3. The Latin derivation of the word "discipline" is *discere*, meaning to teach.

4. The ability to serve as the school's representative for student discipline hearings represents a competency of skill and/or knowledge.

5. In a 2014 mini-study of the primary responsibilities of assistant school principals, one of the three top position tasks was the assistant principal's role of instructional leader.

6. The question, "Tell me about a time you were involved in a problem regarding job satisfaction in the school. What problems did you face and what decisions did you make in this situation?" is a competency-based interview question.

7. Competency-based interviewing places emphasis on the candidate's ability to relate learning from the experience to the position in question.

8. The competencies of achievement and impact of influence were found by Spencer and Spencer as being critical to high levels of success in most demanding leadership positions.

9. A volume of research on school climate supports the finding that positive school climate fosters the presence of positive student behavior.

10. Although indicators of competencies are overt behaviors that illustrate one's ability to accomplish a task effectively, indicators of competencies should not be utilized for purposes of assessing the assistant principal's job performance.

Post–quiz results: Only question #10 is false. I feel confident that you can give yourself a pat on the back.

Summary

How competency-based methodology can serve the goal of improving the role of the assistant school principal is the central focus of Chapter 2. The answer was centered on its potential for providing a framework of the primary tasks, competencies and indicators of competencies of the assistant principal's role. In order for the assistant principalship to be a vital role in the school's administration, it must have a meaningful link to the school's mission, goals and objectives. The point is this: competency-based approaches provide the opportunity to accomplish this vital connection.

Knowing the kinds of knowledge and skills needed in the role of assistant principal serves several purposes of paramount importance. By using competency-based methods to structure the role, the responsibilities are defined so as to allow the assistant principal to use his or her administrative abilities creatively. Performance evaluation target areas and personal growth and development needs can be clearly identified.

Empirical evidence showing the actual responsibilities of the assistant principal indicates that the role in instructional leadership often is missing in position descriptions. Unrelated management activities commonly dominate position descriptions. The chapter presented several examples of models for implementing competency-based methodology in such role functions as the hiring of personnel, interviewing procedures, and positive discipline methods.

We submit that the implementation of competency-based approaches can be used in every activity of the assistant school principal's role. However, the approach is not presented as panacea. Rather, the use of the methodology, when understood and practiced administratively, can lend strength to the role of assistant principal and greatly improve its administrative outcomes. The next chapter centers on the topic of the assistant principal as a student advocate and how he or she can do their best for all students.

The last chapter of the book, Chapter 6, extends the concept of competency-based administration by presenting a compendium of the primary tasks, competencies and indicators of competencies for the position of assistant principal. We include this information in the book since it can serve beneficially for: (1) structuring a meaningful role for the assistant principalship in schools, (2) hiring a candidate for the position of assistant principal, (3) evaluating the performance of an assistant school principal, (4) determining gaps between the actual performance of an assistant principal and meaningful standards for the role, (5) examining the assignments of the assistant principal with reference to the goals and objectives of the school's mission, (6) determining the appropriate administrative methodology for effective practices in the assistant principal's position, (7) setting benchmarks for implementing relevant growth and development activities for the assistant principal, and (8) assessing the appropriate relationship of the work of the assistant principal and the principal of the school.

Discussion Questions

1. Consider the following task of an assistant school principal: To plan and participate in personal professional growth activities. Develop two competencies that would be appropriate for this task, and one indicator of competency for each competency that you choose (e.g., the ability to attend courses, workshops, and conferences directly related to his/her identified needs).

2. Secure a copy of your school assistant principal's position description. Is the description's format competency-based? If not, take a few minutes to rewrite three or more of the assigned responsibilities on the position description using a competency-based format.

3. Like most every administrative procedure, the competency-based method has its critics. Two of the most frequently cited criticisms are as follows: (1) competency-based administrative methods focus on the administrator rather than the clients (students), and (2) competency-based methods focus primarily on skills and knowledge and overlook other "hidden" competencies such as interpersonal skills, accountability and motivation.

   Take a few minutes to examine the chapter contents regarding position descriptions, tasks, competencies and indicators of competency and primary position responsibilities for assistant school principals. Then set forth your thoughts regarding the contentions set forth in criticisms #1 and #2 above.

4. Review the chapter discussion relative to the topic of competency-based interviewing. Then identify three primary differences between competency-based interviewing and other interviewing methods commonly used in hiring interviews.

5. Following are three interview questions/requests asked in the hiring process. Rewrite each of the questions as a competency-based question or request:

   (1) What do you consider to be your personal strengths?

   (2) How do you handle individual differences in student abilities in the classroom?

   (3) Are you a good disciplinarian?

6. Consider the implementation of a competency-based interview. Draft an appropriate question regarding each of the following competencies. For example, an appropriate question for the competency of leadership might be: "Tell me about a time that you faced a problem such as failure of a school committee to make progress on its assigned purposes. What steps did you take to resolve the problem?"

   Draft a question for each of the following competencies: (1) ability to determine growth and development activities for professional personnel, (2) ability to understand and utilize a variety of methods for evaluating the curriculum, (3) ability to supervise and administer student organizations and activities, (4) ability to manage and supervise the school's attendance procedures, and (5) ability to communicate and work cooperatively with members of the school community.

CASE STUDIES

Case 2.1 Something Is Missing Here

The Fairview High School principal, Robert Compos, called assistant principal Al Orlonzo into his office for a personnel performance conference. Fairview School District policies call for the principal's recommendation for merit pay increases toward the end of each school year. Assistant Principal Orlonzo had served in the role for nearly three years and had not been eligible for a merit pay increase during that interim.

"Come in Al," said Principal Compos, "How did it go for you today?" he asked.

"Well," responded Orlonzo, "I got all the kids on the bus and have the parking lot pretty well cleared out. What's up?" he asked.

"It's that time again. I have to send my recommendation on merit to the central district office this week and need to inform you that I am not able to place you on the approval list again this year. Of course, merit consideration calls for performance above the call of duty, as you know. Just doing the job unfortunately isn't enough. One has to shine out above the crowd," said Principal Compos.

"I am greatly disappointed, of course," said Orlonzo. "I thought that I was performing quite well in doing the tasks that you assign to me each week. And, too, I am doing many other things for the school that you might not know all about. My efforts to improve student discipline are not always apparent but I have conferred with all but three teachers on improving the school's discipline activities. Transportation of students is improving as of late and campus safety measures are being attended," he added.

"Oh, I know, I know," answered Principal Compos. "The work that you are doing certainly is satisfactory. But merit is difficult to assess in the work that you do. We can judge the performance of a classroom teacher in different ways including, of course, improved student achievement as demonstrated by test scores. These standards have not been defined for assistant principals."

"Well I would like to follow-up with you on this matter, I just can't think that there isn't something missing here."

Question

1. Examine the case once again and then describe what you consider to be missing here. Be thoughtful and thorough in your response. Determine what is needed to remedy the present negative outcomes. What administrative action, for example, needs to be taken to improve the stature and contributions of the assistant principal's role at Fairview High School?

Case 2.2 Request for Input—Strengthening the Student Activity Program in the High School

Memorandum
To: Randall Craig, Assistant Principal
Columbia High School
From: Brian Scott, Assistant Superintendent of Schools
RE: Request for Input
cc: Gregory Stephens, Principal
Columbia High School

Date: September 25

You will recall that last fall the parent group within several of our schools expressed concern for an extended/improved student activity program especially at the high school level. Parents of students at Columbia High School were quite adamant in this regard. I think that it is imperative that we take some action with specific program recommendations at this time.

I plan to prepare a report on our plans to improve the student activity programs at the October 28 meeting of the school board. Your insights would be especially valuable to me in preparing this report. I would appreciate your recommendations concerning the specifics of program activities, opportunities for student involvement, assignment of sponsors and time schedules.

As you will recall, the survey of student interests last fall turned up little new information. Most felt that athletics were overemphasized and that many students were left out of the sports programs due to the focus on winning. Other expressions of student interests were widespread. If my records are accurate, Columbia High School presently offers the major sports for boys and volleyball, basketball and gymnastics for girls. The debate team and drama class has limited student involvement.

Please know that your recommendations are appreciated. If you have questions, please direct them to me or to my office assistant.

Directions

Assume the role of Randall Craig, assistant principal, and detail the follow-up steps that you would take in response to the assistant superintendent's request. Do not just say, "I would do this or that," rather actually complete the administrative tasks by completing necessary communication such as memos, emails and telephone messages. Avoid saying that I would seek additional information. Rather, seek the information required by using the appropriate communication. It would be expected that you do send a memo to Assistant Superintendent Scott with a detailed description of your recommendations.

References

Boyatzis, R.E. (2009). Competencies as a behavioral approach to emotional intelligence. A conceptual paper. Emerald Group Publishing Limited, Emerald 28. Cleveland, OH: Case Western Reserve University.

Clifton, D.O., & Nelson, P. (1992). *Soar with your strengths*. New York: Dell.

Darling-Churchill, K., Stuart-Cassel, V., Ryberg, R., Schmitz, H., Balch, J., Bezinque, A., & Conway-Turner, J. (2013). *Compendium of school discipline laws and regulations for the 50 states, Washington, D.C. and Puerto Rico*. National Center on Safe Supportive Learning Environments. Available at: http://safesupportivelearning.ed. gov/School-Discipline-Compendium.

Experis Manpower Group (March 19, 2014). *Interview questions checksheet—UK*. From the web: www.experis.co.uk/research-insights/employer-guidance-and-advice/interview-questions-checksheet

Hay Group (1996). *Competencies drive the HR practices* (p. 15). Research sponsored by the American Compensation Association and conducted by the Hay Group, Hewitt Associates, Towers Perrin and William Mercer. Philadelphia, PA: Hay Group.

Head Start and Early Start (December 13–15, 2006). *Establishing a competency-based management framework*. Interdepartmental Committee on Competency-Based Management—Government of Canada. Washington, D.C.: Directors' Institute. English.

Interdepartmental Committee on Competency-Based Management—Government of Canada (December 13–15, 2006). *Establishing a competency-based management framework*. Washington, D.C.: Head Start and Early Head Start Directors' Institute. HHS/AFC/OHS. English.

Norton, M.S. (2013). *Competency-based leadership: A guide for high performance in the role of the school principal*. Lanham, MD: Rowman & Littlefield Education.

Norton, M.S., & Kriekard, J.A. (1987). Real and ideal competencies for the assistant principal. *NASSP Bulletin*, 71(501), 23–30.

Skiba, R., Reynolds, C.R., Graham, S., Sheras, P., Conoley, J.C., & Garcia-Vazquez, E. (2006). *Are zero tolerance policies effective in the schools?* Washington, D.C.: American Psychological Association Zero Tolerance Task Force.

Spencer, L.M. Jr., & Spencer, S.M. (1993). *Competence at work: Models for superior performance*. New York, Wiley & Sons.

ThinkWise, Inc. (2007). *Using a competency-based approach: Linking core competencies to your business strategy*. Grand Rapids, MI: ThinkWise. From the web: http://thinkwise.com/Files/Competency-Based-Approach-Whitepaper.pdf.

The Assistant Principal as a Student Advocate

Primary chapter goal:

To help each assistant school principal and those individuals who aspire to the role of a school administrator ask themselves the question: Am I truly doing what is in the best interests of each individual student toward the goal of helping them reach their full potential?

The Story of Merton

Merton was an eighth-grade student at Whittier Junior High School who once again found himself sitting in the assistant principal's office. Merton's social studies teacher had dismissed him from the room for disruptive behavior. All of Merton's teachers at one time or other had recommended that he be removed from their classes. His math teacher had suggested his suspension. Merton's tardy and absentee record was troublesome. With the exception of his grades in art class, his academic record was unsatisfactory as well. Merton exhibited all of the behavioral characteristics of a potential school dropout.

The assistant principal, Hazel Hurst, had made several calls to Merton's parents and had met in conferences with Merton's mother on three different occasions. Calling the parents again on the same matter did not appeal to Mrs. Hurst at this time. As she sat with Merton in the office, she looked at his last report card and noticed the grade of "C" in art.

"Well, Merton," she said, "You seem to like art. Is that something you like to do?"

"Yeah," Merton replied.

"Do you do any art work at home?" asked Mrs. Hurst.

"My room in the basement at home is full of it," Merton replied. "I mostly do some water color paintings and I like to sculpture," he offered.

Mrs. Hurst asked Merton if he would be willing to bring a few of his art works to her office tomorrow and he agreed to do so. In the meanwhile, she informed Merton's teachers that she would be working personally with Merton for the next two days. She asked Merton's art teacher if she was available after school to discuss Merton's situation.

The art teacher recommended several art publications that might be of interest to Merton. However, she doubted that Merton would appreciate the material since she had never heard him say "thank you." In addition, the math teacher, social studies teacher and the English teacher suggested several activities for Merton that tied art to their subject areas. For example, the English teacher had Merton writing compositions about modern art. The social studies teacher had Merton study several publications on the history of art and several biographies of famous artists. The math teacher gained the student's interest in a book on mathematics and culture.

As a result of these support efforts, several pieces of Merton's artwork were displayed in the school's entry display case. One sculpture was a scottie dog modeled exactly to scale. Surprisingly enough, Merton started to come to school on time and was in attendance on a daily basis.

By the beginning of the second semester of school, Merton's class grades greatly improved. Merton presented Mrs. Hurst with a sculpture of the school's eagle mascot. Reportedly, he was elected as the class representative to the school's student council as a ninth-grader. The art teacher asked Merton to be her assistant.

We cannot say just what Merton's future might have been if one caring assistant principal and several teachers had not taken the time and effort to support him at a troublesome time in his school career. However, it is quite likely that Merton would have dropped from school and his potential contributions to society most likely lost. Fortunately, we have many "Hazel Hurst's" in our schools today who reveal their student advocacy traits on a daily basis.

Did You Have a Favorite Teacher During Your School Years?

Think about a teacher or teachers from your school years who you consider as the best that you experienced. We want you to take a few minutes to write down the things that put them on your "best teacher" list. We'll wait for you. List as many things that you can that describe the teacher(s).

Now, take your list and check it against the list of traits that follows. Check each entry on your list that is very similar to one on the list below (Norton et al., 2012):

- **Student centered**—one who was committed to helping me reach my potential.
- **Caring**—one that truly cared about me.
- **Respect for students**—one that revealed respect for students as individuals.
- **What's best for students**—one whose decisions were made in the best interests of students.
- **Student rights**—one who stood up for students' rights as individuals.
- **Good listener**—one who made an effort to see things from the student's perspective.
- **Each student was an individual**—one who viewed each student as a contributor according to his/her potential.
- **Discipline**—one who implemented non-punitive discipline; discipline was a learning experience.

The Assistant Principal Advocacy Traits Assessment

The entries set forth in the foregoing paragraph illustrate eight traits of student advocates. If you found that four or more of the traits paralleled those on your best-teacher's list, authorities believe that these traits are a mirror for revealing your personal advocacy behaviors as well. We want to re-check this contention by asking you to take the Assistant Principal Advocacy Traits Assessment (APATA) that follows. Find a time when you can take 20 minutes to complete the assessment. Just follow these directions.

Directions: Respond to each of the following scenarios according to your personal beliefs and dispositions. For each case, check the one best response that is closest to your opinion as the one that you would implement as the assistant school principal. This isn't a test; rather this is an opportunity for you to state what you really believe. Avoid skirting the answer with such thoughts that this incident is outside your current administrative role or saying that you would need more information. No one else will see your results, so be yourself; be sure that your responses reflect you and your opinions.

1. The school board in the school district in which you serve as an assistant principal is considering the adoption of a student retention policy that the state has recommended for schools. In brief, the policy states that any third-grade student who does not test at grade level in reading and mathematics by the end of

the school year be retained. The school board meets to discuss this matter next Tuesday and you plan to attend. There is a time for those in attendance to speak to the matter. Which one of the actions below are you most likely to take?

____a. Attend the meeting to learn about the various thoughts on this matter, so that you can be better prepared to handle the policy if it is passed by the school board.

____b. Stand and suggest that the reading and arithmetic cut-off scores for retaining a student be lowered from 2.9 to 2.5 to allow more students to move on to grade 4.

____c. Stand and suggest that students not meeting the cut-off score of 2.9 be required to take summer school classes in these subjects.

____d. Stand and speak against the adoption of the proposed policy, noting that it would actually be detrimental to student academic achievement and other aspects of student behavior.

2. Assistant principal Roland Hart was new to Ostenberg Elementary School. He had served as an elementary school teacher in another school district for eleven years before accepting the position at Ostenberg Elementary. The selection team was impressed with Roland's record in the area of curriculum and instruction. He had chaired the intermediate grade curriculum revision team in his prior position. At the first meeting of the Ostenberg faculty in the fall, Roland was introduced and asked to say a few words. He expressed his enthusiasm for the new administrative role and spoke briefly about his concept of an inclusive school. He emphasized that he favored an inclusive school concept that centered on including students with special needs in general education classrooms. During the next six weeks Roland worked diligently to implement the inclusive concept at Ostenberg Elementary. Although he had the support of the school principal, rumblings among the faculty members were evident. The contentions centered on the statement that special needs students were taking too much time and distracting time being given to the other students in the class. Others indicated that they were not qualified to teach special needs students. It became obvious that something had to be decided about the inclusive concept. Roland met with the school principal on the matter. The principal was clear that he would support him regarding the decision that Roland wanted to relate to the faculty at the meeting next Tuesday. Assume the role of Roland Hart. Which action below will you most likely take?

____a. Tell the faculty that you understand their feelings on the matter and that the inclusive concept will be discontinued.

____b. Tell them that in-service activities for successful student inclusiveness programs will continue and that inclusiveness ultimately will be in the best interests of all students.

____c. Point out that you will recommend that inclusive classrooms be restricted to no more than twenty-two students so that all students can receive more attention.

3. A middle school student was found distributing cigarettes to students on the school campus. The student argued that he had found the cigarettes in a package in the street on the way to school. This matter was sufficient to approve a search of the student's locker. No other tobacco was found. What actions are you going to take?

____a. Do nothing, no harm no foul.

____b. Recommend three days of suspension according to the school policy of substance abuse items on campus.

____c. Meet with the student to gain his full story on the matter. Try to determine an activity that would help the student understand the problems of having certain things such as cigarettes in the hands of students.

____d. Demand that the boy identify others who accepted the cigarettes so that justice can be served.

4. A senior high school student, Monty Carmel, has a record of a successful student all during his high school years. He has been on the honor roll consistently, president of his class, and captained the basketball and track teams of the school. During the past few weeks, however, Monty seems to have withdrawn from class participation and interest in school generally. Just recently, he asked to be released from the position of activities club president, a club for which you, the assistant school principal, serve as sponsor. At the last club meeting, you confront Monty by saying that you have noted his unusual behavior and if he has something to say to just get up and say it. Monty accepted the "challenge" and, in brief, stood and pointed out experiences within the school that he considered to be questionable. He commented that high school graduation was only one semester away and at the graduation ceremonies some speaker most likely would stand and tell the graduates that they were the future of the nation. Yet, he continued, as seniors we are limited to using certain facilities in the school without the overseeing of some adult teacher or go to the bathroom without carrying a pass and must continue to follow myriad school rules that were first initiated in grade school. If the goal of this school is to prepare us to assume a leadership role in society and take responsibility for our own actions, I think that our school has failed in preparing us to do so. You asked me to get up and say what I am feeling and I have done so said Monty. As the school assistant principal and club sponsor, what would you say or do at this time?

____a. Do nothing, Monty has just let off steam and it's all over.

____b. Take a strong stand. Let Monty know that the school has rules and they apply to him as well.

____c. Give immediate attention to Monty's thoughts and feelings about how the school truly is providing experiences and opportunities for students to learn about such things as initiative and responsibility.

____d. Take Monty aside and assure him that the school is doing the best for him and that he will appreciate his years in school as life goes on.

5. Which experience or outcome below do you believe would bring you the most position satisfaction?

____a. As assistant school principal, seeing that your concept of an inclusive school was ultimately successfully implemented in your school.

____b. Being named assistant school principal of the year by the state administrators' association.

____c. Witnessing Monty Carmel's award by the Community Cooperative Club as the high school's athlete with the highest academic grade point average.

____d. Getting your article on the topic of student retention published in the national journal of elementary education.

6. Your school district has a procedure administered by the central business office for transferring books from one school to the other. A form has to be completed by the school that wants to send extra books to another school that needs them as soon as possible. Delivery days for picking up and delivering books usually are once a week but overall the transfer process can take up to four weeks to complete. As the assistant school principal who needs the thirty books for a reading class, the waiting period of transfer is problematic; teachers and students face being without books for too many days. You decide to go to the business manager and ask to expedite the transfer. You will complete the transfer form, but just pick up the available books at the other school and take them to your school on the same day. When you present the idea to the business manager, he says, "No way, we have procedures around here and they are intended for you as well! Furthermore, if I hear any more about your wanting to circumvent the district's procedures, you and I will see ourselves in the superintendent's office!" Which entry that follows is closest to what you would do or say?

____a. I would say, "Let's go, my students need books now."

____b. I would leave well enough alone. My job could be in jeopardy.

____c. I would pick up the needed books anyway and take them to my school.

____d. I would ask the teacher to improvise as best she could at this time.

7. A sophomore student in your school is sent to your assistant principal's office for "insubordination." The English teacher's weekly class assignment was for the student to write a composition on today's political scene. According to

the student, he told the teacher that he was not interested in politics and wondered if he could write a paper on drones. Her response was negative. She said that this is not a science class and that all students were writing on the assigned topic. It would not be fair to let me make an exception. "My answer was, Why not?" said the student.

"Then she asked me to leave the classroom and go to your office." It was the last class period of the day. The student was dismissed and asked to report back to your office the first thing in the morning. You went to the teacher's room right after the last class and asked her about the class assignment and her objectives for the student assignment. She said that her primary objective in the assignment was to check the correct uses of grammar in written work. Which of the following entries is closest to your recommendation at this point?

____a. Be an advocate for the teacher's methods and not get involved in the way she teaches.

____b. Inform her that you will direct the student to follow her assignment requirements. Students are not to be the decision makers in regard to what is to be required in the classroom.

____c. Recommend that the teacher be flexible in the assignment and note that her purpose of correct use of grammar could be accomplished just as well by allowing the student to write on a topic of personal interest.

8. Your school holds a program improvement meeting weekly. As the assistant school principal for curriculum and instruction at Wilson High School, you moderate these sessions. When you entered the meeting room, the school principal and a small group of teachers were discussing Sally Miller. Sally was picked up over the weekend in a car with others. The police found marijuana in the car and some evidence of other substance abuse paraphernalia. The principal said that Sally most likely would be given a school suspension of thirty days starting immediately after the police had reported on the matter. One of the teachers in the group asked if Sally was now at home or in jail. The principal said that he really did not know. What do you say or do, if anything?

____a. Keep out of these matters. Let the police do their job.

____b. Move to the rostrum and open the curriculum and instruction faculty meeting. Instructional improvement remains as first priority.

____c. Ask the principal to open the faculty meeting and then make a call to Sally's parents. Ask what you might do.

____d. Ask the principal if he could speak with you for a minute. Remind him of the requirements for student rights and due process in these cases. Suggest that Sally and her parents be contacted and a hearing process be administered.

9. The teachers' association in your state sent a recent memorandum to all local school boards that recommended the school board's consideration of a

teacher-talent model of school administration. As assistant school principal in the school district, you received the memo as well. Apparently your school board has placed this matter on the agenda for the next school board meeting and has asked all school principals and local teachers' association representatives to attend. Your school principal informed you that he will be in attendance and hoped that you would plan to attend as well. What action, if any, will you take at this time on this matter?

_____a. Wait for the meeting and see what's going on.

_____b. Take specific steps to do some research and find out more about the topic of teacher-led schools.

_____c. Respond to the school principal with some comments opposing the idea.

_____d. Respond to the school principal with some comments that "we seem to be doing ok as we are now."

10. You are in attendance at the parent–teacher organization for your school. As the assistant school principal, you attend all of these meetings if at all possible. Mrs. Scott, the school principal, is away from school unfortunately suffering from the flu. At one point in the meeting, one parent in attendance commented on the unfairness of the discipline procedures being used by the school. She stated that her son was given a much more severe "punishment" for the very same violation that another student committed two days before. What most likely would be your actions/behavior at this point and time?

_____a. Stand and respond briefly to the point that we always try to treat the same violation the same with each and every student.

_____b. Stand and say that you do remember something about the cases but will need to go back and review the cases and get back to the parent.

_____c. Stand and respond briefly that the school has identified those factors that must be considered by the administration and teachers when addressing a disciplinary problem. For example, the frequency, type, and magnitude of previous misbehaviors by the student come into play. We give serious consideration to such questions as "the extent to which the disciplinary decision will be a learning experience for that particular student."

APATA Answers and Scoring Directions

The answers 1d, 2b, 3c, 4c, 5c, 6a, 7c, 8d, 9b, and 10c tend to reflect the actions of administrators who are student advocates. To calculate your advocacy score, multiply the number of entries that you answered correctly by ten. For example: 7 correct × 10 = 70.

Your score reveals the following:

100–90   You most likely could write the remainder of this chapter. You have a very good grasp of advocacy as it applies to student relations.

89–80   You have a good understanding of the traits that define a student advocate. You most likely are already applying these traits in your everyday practice.

79–70   You demonstrate substantial evidence of understanding the concept of student advocacy. Give thought to the nature of your applications of this knowledge and witness the positive student outcomes.

69–Below   The following section of the chapter will serve to explain advocacy traits in more detail. Give the section your full concentration and "experiment" by applying the concept in practice. Both you and your students will appreciate the positive results.

Let's examine each answer given for the APATA assessment. The following section considers each of the ten assessment scenarios and briefly sets forth the rationale for the selected answer.

Response to Scenario 1: Response "d," stand and speak against the adoption of the proposed policy, is the policy that a true student advocate would follow. Non-promotion does not increase learning. In fact, students that are retained in grade achieve less than if promoted to the next grade. Additionally, such characteristics as socialization and motivation are negatively influenced by retention. Students who are retained in grade commonly are school dropouts later on.

Response to Scenario 2: Response "b" represents the student advocate in action. Standing up for what one believes and standing tall when facing negative pressures is a required trait of a student advocate. Responses "a" and "c" for the most part are cop-outs. Student advocacy requires courage. We take this position knowing that student advocates can indeed be wrong. However, in Scenario 2, Roland Hart's concept had not been given a fair chance to succeed. In the real case that Scenario 2 represents, teachers in the school found that the inclusive concept became more and more successful. Student performance scores increased over time and teachers developed new skills in working with a diversified group of students.

Response to Scenario 3: Response "c," meet with the student to get the full story on the matter, is the preferred answer of a student advocate. One of the primary traits of a student advocate is that he or she is a good listener. Student advocates listen to students in order to determine ways to make the situation a learning experience for the student. Helping a student truly learn by their mistakes results in the development of more positive attitudes and encourages personal responsibility.

Response to Scenario 4: Response "c" is most appropriate. Once again, listening and giving credibility to the thoughts of students are represented in the actions of the assistant principal. School leaders foster initiative, responsibility and leadership in students by providing opportunities for them to implement these traits. Is your school promoting or restricting such opportunities? The student advocate is able to see things from the student's viewpoint. Kowalski and others (1992) asked a population of school principals to identify factors that they considered most important in selecting new teachers. Twenty-one factors were listed with ratings from 1–low to 5–high. The top factor in the listing was "respect for students" with a statistic of 4.94. We submit that "respect for students" is high on the list of assistant school principal advocates as well.

Response to Scenario 5: Response "c" centers on a student's success; others tend to center on the assistant principal's recognitions and rewards. Student advocates gain the most satisfaction when they witness the success of students. The student advocate is committed to helping each student succeed.

Response to Scenario 6: Response "a" represents the proactive attitude and courage of a true student advocate. The assistant school principal in this scenario is willing to place himself or herself in "jeopardy" to support students and their right to learn. Student advocates do follow school and school district policies and regulations, but are first to question existing regulations that are detrimental to the best interests of students. The assistant principal might well have put his or her position in danger by confronting an individual in a higher office. The assistant principal discussed the matter with his principal and was supported in his request to confer with the school superintendent on this matter. In the actual case on which this scenario is based, the school superintendent readily endorsed the assistant principal's request to change the book transfer so that books could be received by students within two days of any request.

Request to Scenario 7: Response "c" shows an understanding of the need to consider the students individually and their interests in implementing learning activities. Student advocates emphasize learning as opposed to stressing compliance (Haberman, 1995). Neither of the other options, "a" or "b," is student centered. As indicated by the assistant principal's recommendation to the teacher, her objectives for making the assignment could be accomplished as easily by permitting flexibility on the part of students.

Response to Scenario 8: Response "d" is most appropriate in this situation. The school principal had not acted officially on this matter; actual suspension was pending. In most every state, the suspension of students for more than three days requires a hearing in the fairness of due process. The assistant principal helped the principal in this matter by providing his/her knowledge of suspension and due process in these matters. "Due process is best defined as fairness. Before taking the rights away from any student, school officials must provide fair procedures of due process for that student" (Norton et al., 2012, p. 89). Response "a" certainly is not in the best interests of the student and response "b" does little in demonstrating the advocacy trait of student support regardless of the situation.

Response to Scenario 9: Response "b" demonstrates another important trait of the student advocate. The student advocate has a research-positive attitude. He or she is a consumer, distributor and implementor of quality empirical and basic research. All of the other three responses fall short of what is needed in this case. Attending a meeting when an important administrative change is to be discussed calls for much more leadership than just showing up or responding to a memo of importance before knowing as much as possible about the topic at hand. In order to be a contributing administrator at the forthcoming meeting, the assistant principal must do much more than merely show up. A decision looms important when it has the potential of changing the school's organization and your position as assistant principal. Important to the student advocate is the fact that school organization has many implications for the students in the school. Doing some research and finding out as much as possible about the topic of teacher-talent administrative models are positive steps by the assistant principal at this time.

Response to Scenario 10: Response "c" is the advocate's best response at this open meeting. The brief response was intended to underscore the need to take all factors into consideration when making decisions relative to student discipline. Is the student aware of the behavior expected of him or her? The aggravating and mitigating factors of the case must be considered. For example, the previous pattern of misconduct of the student, the ability of the student to understand the potential consequences of his/her behavior, and the need to make the decision outcomes a learning experience for the student are individual considerations as opposed to the same "punishment" for the same violation concept (Norton et al., 2012). The response of the assistant principal in Scenario 10 gave a factual response to the parent's concern without inducing a further discussion of the personal cases of the students.

Student Advocacy in Relation to the Assistant Principal's Role as a Learning Leader

Previously we discussed the competency-based tasks, competencies and indicators of competency as related to the assistant principal's responsibilities as a learning leader. In the following sections of the chapter we give special attention to how these tasks are implemented and how the desired results are achieved. Our previous discussion of planning and organizing looms important here. An unorganized school without student-oriented procedures is a school heading for failure. The assistant school principal must be an effective leader in creating a school climate that facilitates teaching and learning. Among the necessary administrative considerations for fostering a learning atmosphere is a healthy school climate, assured safety, and orderly campus. Maintaining appropriate student behavior on the campus and in the classroom is on the front page of an advocate's list of things to do.

We will discuss the "how" of this accomplishment in the following section. In any case, the student advocate keeps the welfare of the students foremost in mind. In the next section, we recommend that you use a magic wand to create a positive climate in your school. If you have lost yours, then we do provide several other strategies for improving the climate in your school.

School Climate: What Difference Does It Make?

There is sufficient empirical and basic research to support several major benefits of positive school climates. We submit that one of the most direct ways to improve your students' academic achievement is to implement practices that result in a healthy school climate. We also contend that the assistant school principal's leadership affects school climate either positively or negatively according to the extent that climate improvement behaviors and activities are or are not in place in his or her school activities

Here is what a few authorities in the field have to say about the importance of school climate for students and student learning.

- A positive climate improves student achievement and a sense of belonging. We know that important factors in a positive school climate are also significant mediators of learning: empowerment, authentic engagement, self-efficacy, and motivation. (William H. Hughes, Director of Leadership, and others. National School Climate Center: Publications, April 19, 2014)

- School climate is the holistic context of life, vigor and quality of the social connectedness, physical elements, and supportive practices that nurture inclusion and safeness. (Coulston and Smith, Brown University. National School Climate Center: Publications, February, 2013)

- Developing and sustaining high-quality school climates are deeply tied to strategies emerging from dropout prevention research . . . This research conducted across several decades has revealed not only the at-risk factors most often associated with students who drop out, but also a broad range of strategies that, in combination, go a long way toward meeting the needs of students, particularly those at risk of dropping out. (Duckenfield and Reynolds, National Dropout Prevention Center, April 19, 2014)

- Studies find that it [positive school climate] decreases absenteeism, suspensions, substance abuse, and bullying, and increases students' academic achievement, motivation to learn, and psychological well-being . . . It can even mitigate the negative effects of self-criticism and socioeconomic status on academic success. (Vickie Zakrzewski, in *How to Create a Positive School*

Climate, August 21, 2013, p. 1. Zakrzewski is the education director of the Greater Good Science Center, Berkeley, CA.)

■ A growing body of research shows that school climate strongly influences motivation to learn and improve academic achievement. When school members feel safe, valued, cared for, respected and engaged, learning increases. (California Department of Education, 2013: Positive School Climate, *Safe and Supportive Schools*. California Department of Education, Sacramento, CA.)

A major study of school climate, *A Climate for Academic Success*, by Adam Voight, Gregory Austin and Thomas Hanson (2013), concluded that the study added to the growing body of evidence that suggests that school climate is one of the factors that differentiates schools that succeed and those that do not. In addition, the authors stated that their climate study indicated that a school's climate may have "more" to do with its success than resources at its disposal and "that a positive school climate is an asset for all schools, serving all types of students across demographic spectrums" (p. 28).

What Assistant School Principals Must Do to Help Improve the School's Climate

The following competencies are suggested for you to initiate program activities with the goal of improving the climate of your school. Following the information set forth in Box 3.1, what you could do to accomplish these competencies will be discussed.

Box 3.1 Tasks, Competencies and Indicators of Competencies Regarding the Improvement of the School's Climate

Task

1.0 To provide leadership in the implementation of program activities that promote the development of a positive climate for the school.

Competency

1.1 Ability to assess and evaluate the status of the school's climate.

Indicators of Competency

1.1.1 Has knowledge of the assessment instruments available for possible assessment of the school's climate.

1.1.2 Evaluates the results of climate assessments and analyzes the results relative to areas of climate strengths and areas of apparent weaknesses.

1.1.3 Examines and evaluates the similarities and differences of the climate assessments designed for parents, students and teachers.

1.1.4 Discusses climate assessment results with all appropriate parties and gains their feedback relative to the status of the results.

Competencies

1.2 Ability to use a variety of strategies to examine the school's climate.

Indicators of Competency

1.2.1 Uses small groups of people within the school and without the school to examine the school's climate.

1.2.2 Examines the literature for successful strategies for assessing the school's climate.

1.2.3 Gains the services of outside "consultants" or other qualified individuals to conduct climate discussion sessions or serve as interviewers to get feedback on the school's climate.

1.2.4 Uses a variety of ways to gain information about the school climate including such strategies as focus groups, interviews, observational methods, PTO members and surveys.

Competency

1.3 Ability to cooperate with the school principal, teachers and support staff in the creation of a shared school vision or re-examining the current relevance of the school's present mission statement.

Indicators of competency

1.3.1 Brings the school community together to create a vision of school climate that best will create a learning culture in the school.

1.3.2 Cooperates with the faculty and support staff in implementing the shared vision.

1.3.3 Plans and schedules appropriate climate assessments for the purposes of evaluating improvement results and administering interventions suggested by assessment results.

Assessing Instruments for Determining the Status of School Climate

If you simply type in the words "school climate assessments instruments" on the search engine of your computer, you will find numerous references concerning surveys and other strategies for assessing your school's climate. It is beyond the scope of this chapter to attempt to describe them all, but several examples of such instruments are described in the following section.

In deciding on a survey instrument to use for your climate assessment, several factors should be considered. For example, is the survey to be completed by students, faculty members, parents and other members of the school community or is it being administered to just one of these groups? In some cases, a question that could easily be answered by a faculty member might not be appropriate for a parent to attempt to answer. When you want to compare your school's climate results with other schools in the state or nation, you'll want to know if state and national norms are available for the instrument. Has the instrument been validated? Has it proven reliable? What was its sample size and how recent are its norms?

After synthesizing many of the various climate survey instruments and studies of climate assessment, four major climate areas tend to dominate: The school's physical safety, interpersonal relationships of those within the school and relations with parents, teaching and learning practices and outcomes, and the actual physical environment of the school.

Descriptions of Climate Surveys Available to You for Administration

We previously noted that we would more than fill the remaining pages in this chapter if we tried to list all of the available climate instruments available to you. Four such instruments are described as follows:

1. *The School Climate Quality Analytic Assessment Instrument (SCAI)*. The instrument includes eight factors of climate including physical appearance, faculty relations, student interactions, leadership/decision, discipline environment, learning/assessment, attitude and culture, and community relations. Within each major factor, the participant checks one of three level responses, Level 3 high, Level 2 middle or Level 1 low. However, two middle marks are possible if one's answer falls between low and middle or middle and high. For one major factor relating to attitudes and culture, the participant has the following three choices: **High**—School has a sense of vision that is shared by the staff, **Middle**—School has a set of policies, a written mission but no adhesive vision. **Low**—School has policies that are used inconsistently. The Alliance for the Study of School Climate (ASSC) designed the instrument in 2001. It is located at California State University, Los Angeles, CA.

2. *The Comprehensive Assessment of School Environments (NASSP, 1987). School Climate Surveys (National Association of Secondary School Principals)*. This school

survey is among the most commonly used assessment instruments administered in schools today. NASSP is headquartered in Reston, Virginia.

3. *The Comprehensive School Climate Inventory (CSCI)* is a national climate survey that provides an in-depth profile of your school community's particular strengths and needs. It can be administered to students, parents and school personnel. It has been empirically validated and used in thousands of schools nationally. The instrument has twelve dimensions that include safety, teaching and learning, interpersonal relations, and institutional environment. Participants are to answer each entry on a scale of strongly disagree to strongly agree. A sample entry is: "Adults in my school treat students with respect."

The National School Climate Center, located in New York, should be contacted for additional information.

4. *The Organizational Climate Description Questionnaire—Revised Elementary (OCDQ-RE)* was revised by Hoy and Tarter in 1997. The survey instrument utilizes four climate prototypes to assess a school's climate: open, engaged, disengaged and closed. For example, an open climate is one in which high morale is evidenced by the staff, personal relationships among faculty personnel are positive and the faculty is able to resolve problems in a cooperative manner. On the other hand, a closed climate is evidenced by the low morale of the staff; communication is limited thus problems are not easily resolved. The instrument is discussed in detail in the book by Hoy and Tarter entitled *Healthy Schools* (1997).

You might consider designing your own climate survey instrument. Such instruments need not be lengthy. For example, let's design a brief climate survey to be administered to the students of your school. We will use the four major climate factors of the school's physical safety, interpersonal relationships within the school, teaching and learning practices and outcomes, and the actual physical environment of the school (see Box 3.2.)

Box 3.2 Student Survey of School Climate

Directions: Use the following scale to assess your students' perceptions of each of the entries on the climate assessment scale: 5—Always, 4—Frequently, 3—Sometimes, 2—Seldom, 1—Never. Circle the rating that applies for each entry.

A. The School's Physical Safety

1.   I feel safe when inside the school building as well as on the campus.

    5 4 3 2 1

2. Student harassment and bullying are being practiced by some students in our school.

    5 4 3 2 1

3. Students in our school are fully informed as to what to do in case of school emergencies.

    5 4 3 2 1

4. I am treated respectfully by other students in the school.

    5 4 3 2 1

5. If I had a problem or concern regarding a particular student at my school, I would feel comfortable talking to him or her about it.

    5 4 3 2 1

B. Interpersonal Relationships

1. Relationships among the teachers and students in our school are positive.

    5 4 3 2 1

2. I am respected as an important individual by my teachers.

    5 4 3 2 1

3. The principal and assistant principal of my school know me by name.

    5 4 3 2 1

4. Students in our school are involved in the planning and implementation of school matters that effect them directly.

    5 4 3 2 1

5. I feel that the school administrators and teachers in our school are truly interested in my personal interests and needs.

    5 4 3 2 1

C. Learning Practices and Outcomes

1. My teachers work with me to find the best ways that I learn.

    5 4 3 2 1

2. I am made aware of my learning progress and what to do for personal improvement.

    5 4 3 2 1

3. The environment in our school's classrooms is positive for learning.

    5 4 3 2 1

4. The school's stated mission of "student learning as a priority" is the primary focus of our classroom teachers.

    5 4 3 2 1

5. When students in the school need academic help, they feel that they can get it.

    5 4 3 2 1

D. The Physical Environment of the School

1. Our classrooms, shops and campus grounds are safe, clean and attractive.

    5 4 3 2 1

2. I am always pleased to show friends and visitors our school campus and its facilities.

    5 4 3 2 1

3. If a parent or new student enters our school for the first time, they would be positively impressed with the school's appearance.

    5 4 3 2 1

4. The classroom facilities in the school are such to foster an environment for learning.

    5 4 3 2 1

5. Students in our school are positively active in keeping our school clean and free of graffiti.

    5 4 3 2 1

The most productive school climate instruments are ones that you and your staff design and implement. Such assessment instruments tend to fit the specific interests and needs that match your school situation. In evaluating the assessment results, give serious consideration to what the results are telling you, not just that the results are good or bad. Deal with the most important results at the outset. Are certain "congratulations" in order? What interventions and/or improvements become priorities on your work schedule? If problems exist relating to physical safety, take care of these immediately by reporting them to the proper office with accompanying photos. You respect students and you respect their safety.

How the Student Advocate Establishes a Learning Culture in Your School

School administrators who are student advocates are committed to creating a school culture that provides optimal opportunities for teachers to teach and students to learn (Norton et al., 2012). In accomplishing this commitment, they concentrate on maintaining a well-organized school, keeping a safe school environment for students and school personnel, and creating an orderly, purposeful, businesslike climate that facilitates a learning culture within the school (Lezotte & McKee-Snyder, 2011).

Previously, we noted that research has demonstrated that school climate strongly influences motivation to learn and improve academic performance. When school members feel safe, valued, cared for, respected and engaged, learning increases (California Department of Education, 2013). A learning school culture requires an orderly environment. The student advocate works diligently to have things go right and but is prepared to act when things go wrong. As previously noted, your diligence is reflected in your preparedness for emergencies and serious acts of violence.

In positive learning cultures, students and faculty demonstrate personal respect. Students are polite, considerate and the school is void of chaos and confusion. As an assistant principal, you'll have to work hard to prevent serious misconduct. You will need to be proactive in responding to serious violations based on school standards and sound behavior principles. In doing so, student advocates work to extend their personal connections with the student body and personnel of the school. They are instructed in ways to participate in peer mediation and conflict resolution. Conflicts are bound to occur in schools with open climates as well as schools with closed climates. In open climates, however, communication lines are understood and used. Thus, when conflicts occur, they are more easily resolved. Those students in the upper grades in elementary school can serve to mentor younger students as well as serve as tutors and examples of proper behavior.

The Student Advocate Fosters a Learning Culture First of All by Working to Establish a Learning Climate

"**Safe schools** are ones in which members of the school community are free of the fear of harm, including potential threats from inside or outside the school. The attitudes and actions of students, staff and parents support an environment that is resistant to disruption and intrusion, and enables a constant focus on student achievement" (Ministry of Education, 2008, p. 11). **Caring schools** are supported by a school community that has a strong sense of belonging and has meaningful ways of participating in the improvement of student learning. "A caring school is one in which members of the school community feel a sense of belonging, and have opportunities to relate to one another in positive, supportive ways. All aspects of school life embrace and reflect diversity. The school is an inviting place for students, staff, parents and visitors" (Ministry of Education, 2008, p. 30). **Orderly schools** focus on meaningful learning activities, practice student rights, are proactive in promoting positive student conduct, demonstrate mutual respect, and are administered with competence by qualified, caring school leaders.

Student advocates work toward the adoption and implementation of policies, procedures and practices that promote a safer learning culture. They take the leadership in helping students, faculty and parents develop a code of conduct conducive to a positive learning environment. Students are encouraged to participate in school organizations, such as the student council, that serve to promote an orderly school environment. As a leader in establishing a learning climate in your school, you will take opportunities to teach the school's code of conduct and student expectations.

Steps for Developing Procedures for Student Conduct

Working with other groups in the development of an effective statement of procedures for student conduct most likely will be part of your responsibilities as assistant principal. The following steps might be helpful to you as you work to accomplish this task.

1. Expectations for student conduct will be most effective when all parties, students, parents, school administrators and community representatives participate in their development. Understanding and commitment are enhanced.

2. Plans for disseminating the statement of conduct procedures should be developed and implemented.

3. It is of paramount importance that the conduct procedures be presented and explained to students, parents, and teachers periodically. Students and parents new to the school should be fully informed of the conduct procedures.

4. After being implemented, the effectiveness of the student conduct procedures statement should be assessed. Have violations of conduct been improved? Are changes in the procedures needed?

5. The conduct procedures must be in accord with school board policies and state laws. The school's attorney should review the "completed statement." State laws and school board policies commonly set forth certain standards in this regard.

6. A statement of purpose should introduce the conduct procedures with a focus on establishing a safe, caring and orderly school environment for effective learning program activities for students.

7. The conduct procedures should reflect the importance of positive student behavior. Emphasize the importance of each student conducting themselves in ways that result in school pride and personal self-respect. Provide examples of what students are expected to do relative to acceptable behavior (e.g., self-respect, respect of others, school pride, engagement in learning, maturity and self-reliance, civic responsibility, self-discipline, and acts that give credit to the school and self).

8. Include statements to inform students, parents and staff as to what proper conduct is not (e.g., acts of bullying, harassment, intimidation, physical violence, insubordination, creating unsafe school conditions, illegal acts, substance abuse, possession of weapons, interfering with the learning of others).

9. Insert a statement relative to the severity and frequency of misconduct. Note that each case of misconduct is decided by many factors surrounding the situation.

10. Most student conduct procedures include a statement relating to the school's responsibility for reporting serious breaches of conduct to a variety of individuals and offices (e.g., parents of offender and victim(s), school district officials, police and other agencies as required by law and, in certain instances, all members of the school community). In addition, a section on student rights is essential.

In striving to achieve the goal of a learning climate in your school, you will do well to make prevention a priority. You will work with parents in establishing their responsibilities by encouraging their participation in their child's school life and monitoring their child's activities out of school. Check to see if they have received and read the school's student handbook. Underscore the fact that the goals of a learning school cannot be accomplished without their help. Give them ideas for rewarding their child for exemplifying principles of positive behavior. Find ways to make it easier for parents to report safety concerns and/or violations of conduct, safety issues, or evidence of drug and alcohol abuse. Be specific in letting parents know how they can contact you relative to student problems, school procedures and participation in the school's activities. Make them feel comfortable in "their" school.

You'll need to monitor and evaluate the school environment for evidence of improvement in the school's learning culture. The previous discussion of school climate assessment results is one way of accomplishing this task. Your role and responsibilities as assistant principal will require you to be involved in student activities and foster open communication with students. How do you do this? One way is to gain trust. When you tell students what you are going to do, then do what you say. Celebrate student achievements and recognize them for deeds well done. A brief comment often serves a good purpose and travels a long road. "Nice job, Wilma. I watched you from the school window resolving the conflict between those two fourth-graders." "Clyde, Raymond told Miss Brandt that you took the class homework assignment to him when he was out of school yesterday. I understand that you did so on your own. That certainly was thoughtful of you." "Virginia, your English composition on 'Student Relationships: It's Up to You,' is a work of art. May I read it to the entire class?" "James, this morning's visitor came to my office and told me that you stopped her in the hallway and asked if you could help her find a room. You gave her directions to the office. She is the new director of health services for the school district. That was a very courteous thing that you did."

Snapshot 2.1—The Story of Carly

Carly was a seventh-grade student at Ostenberg Middle School. His elementary school record was troublesome. He was retained in grade 3 for academic and behavioral reasons. At one time he was recommended for special education, but testing results were not indicative of this placement.

Carly commonly was referred to as "Mr. Tardy" due to his school record in this respect. He was not a belligerent troublemaker, rather he was viewed as being apathetic and disengaged from learning. Carly often found himself in the assistant principal's office in school's early hours or by noontime. The general consensus was that Carly would drop out of school soon after the attendance age requirement was fulfilled.

On the most recent occasion, Carly's social studies teacher actually accompanied him to the assistant principal's office. Carly was tardy once again. Once he had taken his seat and the students were given a work assignment, the teacher found Carly with his head down on his desk apparently sleeping.

"He looked as though he was sleeping to me," reported the social studies teacher. "How much longer am I expected to contend with him?" she asked. "He, at least, needs to be placed in our special education program," she offered.

The assistant principal kept Carly in his office for the remaining time of the first class period before taking him to his second period English class. Somehow Carly managed to keep out of the principal's office for the rest of the day.

The next morning the assistant principal decided to drive by Carly's home and perhaps knock on the door to learn if Carly was still in bed or perhaps finishing chores that were assigned by his mother. After a few minutes Carly opened the door but the assistant principal did not enter the home. Carly had a coke bottle in his hand but the assistant principal could see partially filled glasses and liquor bottles on tables all around the room.

Carly's mother and father were still in bed. Carly had not had breakfast and was drinking the contents of the partially filled bottles left from the "party" the night before. His morning nutrition was partially 90 proof.

With the help of the school's social worker and the assistant principal's seeing to it that a nutritional breakfast was prepared for Carly each morning, Carly's attitude and behavior began to change. Social workers saw to it that the home environment was altered and the school's social worker and school nurse gave needed attention to Carly's health and welfare. The school faculty came to understand Carly's situation and worked cooperatively with him to become a successful learner.

The Inclusive School: What Does Student Advocacy Have to Do With It?

The underlying theme of this book is that as an assistant school principal, you'll need to improve your administrative skills if you are to realize real success in that administrative role. Improving your student advocacy skills is no exception. Administrative student advocates extend their services beyond just those students with disabilities, but advocacy must be considered for all students in your school. If you are a normal well-qualified assistant principal, you'll most likely find some tasks difficult to do. Stand by a student who just pushed a teacher? Having a teacher bring a fifth-grader to your office who had a knife in his desk? Perhaps suggesting that a female student that had been picked up for shoplifting not be suspended? Having a parent chastise you for not suspending a student who was bullying her son? You might be reflecting on some similar issues that you faced and had some satisfaction in the way that you resolved them.

The story is told about the school administrator who took his calendar book into his home library each weekend, sat back and thought about each entry of meetings, telephone calls, correspondence, parent conferences, teacher visitations and other activities that he had during the past week. What was the situation or problem that was faced? What went right or what went wrong? Why did it go right or wrong? What might I have done differently in those cases that were not positive? What will I think more about in similar situations in the future? As time went by, the administrator felt more and more satisfied about the outcomes of his actions. Sometimes, he noted, he was even tempted to give himself a pat on the back. In any case, this exercise of self-evaluation, according to this school principal, did more for him regarding personal improvement than any other growth activity in which he had engaged.

You need to ask yourself similar questions. Excuses and the use of "yabuts" are not appropriate for student advocates: "Ya, but this kid is beyond any help that I might provide." "Ya, but I have much more important things to do than deal with her." "Ya, but his parents are the ones that need to take care of their child's problems." "Ya, but he failed to do what I recommended. Let him wake up and deal with the negative outcomes of his own decisions." Student advocates ask two important questions before making decisions about a student problem. How will this decision benefit the student and perhaps other students? Will my recommendations for the student result in a learning experience for the student? Is my decision fair to the student in a way that will lead him or her toward better behavior and a more positive attitude in the future? One thing seems certain: when a decision about a student's status is determined they tend to understand whether or not the decision was made by an individual that truly cared for them. Student advocacy most often shows like a bright lightbulb. In some cases, only you know what was done and how the student was served. Not even the student might be aware of what happened to resolve her problem. But you do, and you'll find that to be quite enough.

We have attempted to illustrate the fact that being a student advocate is much more involved than just liking students. We would submit that all school administrators like students, but not all school administrators are student advocates. The true student advocate practices those moral responsibilities of giving each and every student the very best opportunities to achieve according to his or her potential. They take time in their professional development programs to ask themselves: What evidence can I point to that demonstrates that I am doing what is in the best interests of students? Have I demonstrated the courage necessary for pointing out a policy or administrative regulation that is not in the best interests of students? Can I point to a situation when I stood tall in an attempt to gain a student his or her rights? If I were put on the stand, what could I say about what I actually believe about such matters as student inclusion practices, student retention. student discipline, curriculum decisions, special student needs, and student participation in school program decisions?

We submit that as you do even more to utilize your student advocate traits, your job satisfaction and pride in your accomplishment will increase. In the next chapter, we focus your attention on the assistant school principal as a learning leader.

Summary

Chapter 3 centered on the assistant school principal and his or her responsibilities in serving as a student advocate. You identified your memories of a favorite teacher and thought about why they were placed on your list. Your reasons for listing them were compared with the traits of student advocates. The fact that you knew that your best teachers cared about you was closely tied to the fact that student advocates are student centered and their success is foremost in their mind.

School climate was shown to have positive influences on many aspects of student achievement. As an assistant principal, knowing how to assess your school's climate and evaluating assessment results is imperative. Research has demonstrated clearly that a positive school enhances the accomplishments of school goals and objectives.

The tasks, competencies and indicators of competencies for assistant principals in relation to improving school climate were emphasized. Having knowledge of the various assessment instruments available for use by the school and being competent in the designing of climate assessments were important competencies of assistant principals.

Improving the learning climate of the school by establishing a safe and orderly school environment is among the priority goals of student advocates. Such activities as working with teachers, students and members of the community in developing a statement of procedures for student conduct that sets forth behavioral expectations is essential for achieving an orderly environment.

In the final analysis, the traits of student advocates are revealed in the assistant principal's behaviors and decisions relative to programs of student learning, handling student discipline cases, serving special needs students, programming student activities and other administrative behaviors.

Discussion Questions

1. Go back and retake the APATA that was presented at the outset of this chapter. When you have done so, did your answers take on a different perspective now that you have studied Chapter 3? Why or why not?

2. If your school has not done so, develop a climate survey instrument that you would administer to students, teachers or parents of the school. If you are approved to do so, gain the input from the school faculty and appropriate others in designing the instrument. Decide in advance how the results would be evaluated and disseminated.

3. The chapter context stated that the fact was accepted that all school principals like students, but not all school principals are student advocates. What comments might you make about this contention? Do you agree? Why or why not?

CASE STUDIES

Case 3.1 The Michael Donner Case

Office of William J. Morris, M.D.
Medical Building
Madison, Lafayette
March 14

To: Pat Scott, Principal
Madison Middle School
Madison, Lafayette 20751

Michael Donner will be able to return to school next Monday, March 21, and attend regularly. However, because of his rheumatic heart problem, I would request that you arrange with your staff personnel to see that he has a half-hour rest period in some quiet place in the morning and afternoon.

Thank you for your cooperation in this matter.

William Morris
William J. Morris, M.D.

Attachment from Pat Scott to Amelia Contreas, Assistant Principal
Amelia: Please take care of this. Pat

Directions

You have been asked by the school principal to "take care of this matter." Ordinarily the assistant principal might turn the matter over to the school nurse, who would work with Michael's second and fifth period teachers regarding the half-hour rest period. As a student advocate, what other considerations would be appropriate in this case? For example, what additional information would you like to have? Think about the surrounding implications of this case and set forth in writing what you would do relative to Michael's special needs.

References

California Department of Education (April 3, 2013). *Positive school climate: Safe amd supportive schools.* Sacramento, CA: Author.

Cohen, J., Pickeral, T., & McCloskey, M. (December, 2008/January, 2009). Four factors shape school climate. *Educational Leadership*, 66(4), 29–30.

Coulston, C., & Smith, K. (February, 2013). *School climate and inclusion.* National School Climate Center (NSCC). Providence, RI: Brown University.

Duckenfield, M., & Reynolds, B.P. (2014). *School climate and dropout prevention.* Clemson, SC: Clemson University.

Haberman, M. (1995). *Can star teachers create learning communities?* The Haberman Educational Foundation. Houston, TX: National Center for Teacher Certification Information.

Hoy, W.K., & Tarter, C.J. (1997). *Healthy schools: A handbook for change* (Elementary and Middle School Edition). Thousand Oaks, CA: Corwin.

Hughes, W.H. (2014). *School climate practice briefs.* New York: National School Climate Center.

Kowalski, T.J., McDaniel, P., & Reitzug, U.C. (1992). Factors that principals consider most important in selecting new teachers. *ERS Spectrum,* 10(2), 34–38.

Lezotte, L.W., & McKee-Snyder, K. (2011). *What effective schools do: Re-envisioning the correlates.* Bloomington, IN: Solutions Tree.

Ministry of Education (November, 2008). *Safe, caring, orderly schools: A guide.* British Columbia, Canada: Author, p. 26.

Norton, M.S., Kelly, L.K., & Battle, A.R. (2012). *The principal as student advocate: A guide for doing what's best for all students.* Larchmont, NY: Eye On Education.

Voight, A., Austin, G., & Hanson, T. (2013). *How climate distinguishes schools that are beating the achievement odds* (Department Summary). San Francisco, CA: WestEd.

Zakrzewski, V. (April 21, 2013). How to create a positive school climate. *Greater Good: The Science of a Meaningful Life.* Berkeley, CA: Greater Good.

The Assistant Principal as a Learning Leader

> **Primary chapter goal:**
>
> To underscore the role of the assistant principal as a learning leader and to bring the position into the front line of school purposes.

Chapter 4 centers on the implementation of administrative tasks and competencies and recommends effective procedures for their achievement in practice. Let's begin by considering the competency of establishing a learning culture in the school. One related indicator of competency is that the assistant principal demonstrates this skill by studying and applying the most recent research data related to how students learn. This knowledge looms important in the assistant principal's work with teachers for improving their students' academic performance, designing curriculum and implementing relevant professional development programs.

The Montgomery County Public Schools (1995–2014) has completed an impressive statement of standards for assistant school principals and other administrators relative to professional growth standards that facilitate a vision of teaching and learning shared and supported by the school community. Each standard is accompanied by several "competency" examples of facilitation, articulation, implementation and monitoring that meet the standards, and examples of ones that do not meet the standards. The six standards are set forth in the following section and one "competency" example is included for each standard to illustrate its purposes.

Each assistant principal of a school-based program is an educational leader who promotes success for all students as he/she:

Standard I: assists in facilitating the development, articulation, implementation, and stewardship of a vision of teaching and learning shared and supported by the school community.

Example: Works with teams/departments to facilitate clear understanding of appropriate, measurable goals for student learning, and to align expectations and goals with standards, works with teams/departments to develop plans for monitoring progress toward team/department school goals; assists in monitoring progress.

Standard II: nurtures and sustains a school culture of high expectations, professional growth, and an instructional program conducive to student learning.

Example: Uses classroom observations and monitors formative assessment data to ensure that teachers use instruction that aligns with the school district's curriculum; works with team/department leaders to interpret district curriculum guidelines.

Standard III: promotes success for all students as he/she shares the responsibility for the management of the organization, operations, and resources for a safe, efficient, and effective learning environment.

Example: Supports a master schedule with a balanced program of learning opportunities for all students; assists in monitoring assignment of students to classes/staff that best meet student needs.

Standard IV: promotes success for all students as he/she collaborates with the school staff and other stakeholders including students, families, and community members.

Example: Works with principal/supervisor and team/department leaders to maximize retention of staff who reflect the diversity of the school community.

Standard V: promotes success for all students as he/she models professionalism and professional growth in a culture of continuous improvement.

Example: Assists the principal or supervisor in creating opportunities for staff to assume leadership or expanded roles in the school.

Standard VI: promotes success for all students as he/she understands, responds to, and influences the larger political, social, economic, legal, and cultural context.

Example: Interprets and complies with the school district's policies, regulations and procedures, as well as local, state and federal mandates (e.g., special education, 504, search and seizure, No Child Left Behind); provides opportunities for team/department discussion and understanding.

Empirical and Scientific Research Regarding Student Learning Styles

Various styles of human learning are addressed in the research literature. The **linear learning concept** is characterized by the way most elementary schools are organized and subjects taught. In mathematics, for example, the student works on learning about numbers, then on addition and subtraction, works on the multiplication tables and then learns short division. Learning is viewed as building blocks where by one concept must be "mastered" before the next more advanced step can be taken. On the other hand, **cognitive learning** is more like networking. The student learns by watching, reading, and experiencing some stimuli. Learning is collected in a network fashion. The following definition explains the cognitive learning process. "Cognitive learning can be defined as the process by which one acquires knowledge or skill in cognitive processes. Cognitive processes include reasoning, abstract thinking, decision making, problem solving etc. This information is processed by the brain and later recalled" (Ask.com, April 26, 2014, p. 1).

As you examine the foregoing definition, think about the problems related to student retention in grade. Retention commonly results in having students repeat the same subject material. Shepard and Smith (1989) refer to a recommendation by researcher Penelope Peterson, who proposed that greater teacher knowledge about how children learn might make teachers less ready to see retention as a remedy. As Peterson (2014) suggests, "the challenge for the teacher would become one of accessing and diagnosing the knowledge and abilities of their children to solve problems and then organizing and arranging the learning environment and learning activities to facilitate children's development of that knowledge" (p. 12). Research tells us that students who are permitted to move to the next grade will learn more than if they are retained. A cognitive learner, for example, has collected knowledge and skills that are exhibited later when a new concept serves to connect the stored information and a learning spurt takes place.

In the following section we describe several other learning styles. A **learning style** represents the way a student best acquires and processes concepts and information in different learning situations. Although many authorities in the field contend that individuals differ in how they learn, critics argue that there is no evidence that learning and implementing a student's learning style will indeed produce better achievement outcomes (Pashler et al., 2008). Almost every model of learning styles that has been developed has received critical reviews that commonly point to flawed research. We suggest that action research by the teacher in regard to learning styles appears to be a beneficial activity on the part of teacher student advocates.

Several other learning style models are described as follows:

1. David Kolb's **Experimental Learning Model**, as set forth in his publication, *Experimental Learning* (1984), speaks of concrete experience and abstract conceptualization as related to grasping experience and transforming experience. He identified four learning styles: accommodator, converger, diverger and assimilator. According to Kolb, a learner might prefer one of the four styles depending on their approach using the experimental learning model. For example, the accommodator prefers the hands-on discovery method, challenges theories, and uses feelings as opposed to logic. A converger prefers to work alone, problem-solve and deal with specific problems. A diverger learns best through real life experiences, likes discussion, prefers to observe

rather than do, and likes to work in groups. The assimilator likes theoretical models and graphs, prefers talking about things rather than doing them, and likes to work with numbers (Kolb, 1984).

2. Neil Fleming's (2001–2011) learning style model, referred to as **VARK**, lists four kinds of learning styles: visual, auditory, reading–writing, and kinesthetic or tactile. It is one of the most commonly used models to describe learning styles. The visual model is characterized by the concept that visual learners learn best when seeing is emphasized. Visual aids such as pictures, graphs, symbols, diagrams and others are preferred over the use of lectures. On the other hand, auditory learners gain more via the use of listening. Lectures, group discussions, conversations and audiotapes are most effective for their learning. Learning through experience is best for tactile/kinesthetic learners. The sense of touch and actually doing experiments loom important. "Learn by doing" best describes this style. Reading and writing learning is just that; these learners are prolific readers and they learn additionally by writing about things that they have read about. Rather than trying to learn by watching a film or listening to an instructor's remarks, the reading and writing learner would rather read about it.

3. The **NASSP Learning Style Model** (Keefe, 2005) centers on the concept that learning styles are cognitive, affective and physiological behaviors that indicate how learners learn. Cognitive learning was discussed previously in this section. This style prefers the learning modalities of perceiving, organizing and retaining information. The knowledge gained in grade 3 relative to multiplication facts and multiplication operations is stored in the brain. Nevertheless, insight regarding the ability to do long division may not occur until a later time, perhaps in grade 4. Affective styles, according to Keefe, are dependent on the learner's learning personality or personal motivation approach. The third learning style set forth by Keefe is the psychological style. That is, a student's make-up determines his or her response to learning conditions. Environmental factors such as surroundings, climate, light and sound affect the student's motivational status. How can the teacher determine the learning style of a student? According to Keefe, the learning style can be determined only by observing the student's behavior.

4. **Anthony Gregorc's (2011) model** establishes four learning styles: concrete random, concrete sequential, abstract sequential and abstract random. Concrete perceptions refer to information gained via the five senses of seeing, hearing, smelling, touching and tasting. Abstract perception refers to ideas and concepts that cannot be seen. Sequential refers to a logical or linear organization while random reflects unorganized information. Students with different combinations of the styles learn in different ways. For example, a student with the dominant learning style of concrete sequential is task

oriented, is efficient and likes detail. An abstract sequential student reveals intelligence and analytical abilities, and is capable of working with theoretical concepts.

Our primary purpose of identifying a few of the conceptual models of human learning styles is to emphasize the differences in learners that sit in your school's classrooms every day of the week. The adage "know your students" first and foremost suggests that the teacher should know something about the students they are teaching. Knowing how a student learns best will help the teacher do his or her best in implementing instructional methods that result in improved student performance.

The Assistant Principal Supports Staff Efforts to Determine Individual Student Interests and Instructional Needs

We stress throughout this book that student advocates make learning decisions based on the student's interests and instructional needs. But just how can this objective be met? Here are a few ways that you can help your teachers determine students' interests and needs. The National Research Council (1997) makes these suggestions: (1) "Knowledge about the students will enable the teacher to refine his or her lessons and activities so that they are more effective learning experiences. References to students' interests, backgrounds, knowledge . . . can make the class seem more personal and the material more accessible," (2) "By assessing comprehension levels of a particular subject the teacher can modify his or her own teaching to fit students' needs," and (3) "On the first day of class, hand out a questionnaire that serves to find out the student's background in the subject, any special accommodations the student may need for learning disabilities or special interests that they possess."

One teacher described her strategy for determining a student's needs relative to the subject at hand. She would hand out a list of vocabulary words used commonly in the subject and ask each student to check the words that were unfamiliar to them. She reported that this activity consumed only a few minutes of time but contributed much to the planning of class lessons.

The National Council of Teachers of English (April 27, 2014) sets forth four interesting pre-assessment strategies for assessing student interests and strengths: (1) At the start of a unit, write a letter to students explaining what you want them to know, understand and be able to do in the upcoming unit. Such a strategy can be beneficial in discerning their interest level in the topic as well as their strengths and needs. (2) Use a student survey that asks students about their interests in the topic and their present understanding of the key concepts of the upcoming unit. (3) Ask students to write a one-sentence "truth statement" about an upcoming unit, its interest to them and their knowledge of it. Or ask them what was the most interesting day of your class thus far, and (4) think aloud: Select a portion of a text that you feel illustrates the difficulty that students might have with the text. As you read, interject your impromptu thoughts and explain which words trigger these thoughts (pp. 1–2).

An additional suggestion for identifying students' interests and needs is to ask them to write a paragraph on the topic: "If I had a free day to do whatever I wanted to do, what would I do?" Or, "If I was given free time to read a book, what book or book topic would I choose?" Or, "What was the most interesting and beneficial topic that I studied last year in school?" The surprising information gained through this activity could open suggestions for tying expressed interests directly to the subject presently being taught.

Setting High Expectations in Regard to Student Learning Outcomes

Performance expectations for all learners should be determined; teachers should be certain that the expectations for each student are appropriate for him or her. When appropriate assessments and background information have been evaluated, the teacher or teacher-team should work out the individual educational plan (IEP) needed for the student to progress as a learner. As we have implied in the previous sections on learning styles, assessments and evaluations of the results of the IEP should be monitored. The old adage that "If the student hasn't learned, the teacher hasn't taught" has some credibility here. The adage, although somewhat contentious, does suggest that the teacher's instructional plan is not working and changes need to be considered. High expectations for students have been shown to be positive motivators for student learning, but both the student and the teacher must have a clear understanding of them and just how the expectations reflect the present status of the student's learning and what is to be done in order to meet the learning expectations.

Some students' learning progress is inhibited by factors such as sight and hearing problems, undiagnosed special needs, language differences, visual-perceptual development and other issues. For example, "Some students have a discrepant pattern of abilities; they have severe learning disabilities in one or more areas, yet demonstrate extraordinary strengths in other areas" (Norton et al., 1996, p. 36). A student with a lag in visual-perceptual development has difficulty recognizing objects, and this distortion/confusion of visual symbols poses learning problems for them in almost every subject area, although they may be highly intelligent.

Marzano (September, 2010) makes an important observation of which your teachers should be informed. He states that "In practice, teachers' behaviors toward students are much more important than their expectations. Students cannot know what teachers are thinking, but they do observe how teachers behave—they make inferences on the basis of these behaviors" (p. 2). That is, with low expectancy students teachers make less eye contact, smile less, make less physical contact, and engage in less playful or light dialogue). Marzano believes that teachers can determine their differential treatment of low-expectancy and high-expectancy students simply by noting and recording their behavior toward these two groups of students.

How Does an Assistant School Principal Make Clear His/Her Support of an Inclusive School?

No principal has the magic wand that will implement the inclusive concept in his or her school. Norton et al. (2012) argue that the answer to the question "why inclusiveness?" rests in the stated purposes of schools and why schools exist. Few would oppose the fact that schools exist to educate all students regardless of their status: "an inclusive school is one in which all children, including those with diverse abilities, needs, talents, interests, goals, backgrounds, ethnicities and motivations can learn and come to school wanting to learn" (Norton et al., 2012, p. 34). Without students, schools would not exist. Inclusion from our perspective is not only the placement of students with disabilities in the normal classroom; we view an **inclusive school** as one that includes all children, regardless of their status, in normal classroom settings.

We recommend that you and other members of your school's staff take time to discuss what they believe about such terms as inclusiveness, diversity, excellence, collaboration, learning culture, and student advocacy. How do the members of your school staff define these terms? Is there a collective belief that is revealed in the members' definitions? Is the collective definition of each term one that can be implemented in the thinking, behaviors, and decisions about student learning in our school? As underscored by Falvey and Givner (2005), inclusion is a belief system and not just a set of strategies. It's about attitude and dispositions. It is a vision that drives all decisions and actions by those who subscribe to it.

William Ouchi (1981) speaks of subtlety and intimacy and their importance in building a system's culture. **Subtlety** focuses on studying the situation and then making decisions on the basis of these findings as opposed to rigid rules and regulations. **Intimacy** evolves from the positive interpersonal relationships that are evidenced in the ways people demonstrate concern for the welfare of others. Subtlety and intimacy, according to Ouchi, result in the characteristic of trust. **Trust** is the trait that binds integrity, openness, personal regard, competence, reliability and consistency within the school community.

A Pre-Section Quiz

Directions: Give your answer of true or false for each of the following statements. Avoid just guessing the answer. If you really do not know the answer, just skip that question and go to the next one.

1. In contemporary schools, the often-stated adage that "Failure is not an option" has been replaced by the more meaningful focus of "learning for learning's sake." ___T ___F

2. Empirical evidence and basic research have revealed that parent participation in their child's education in the end does more harm than good. ___T ___F

3. The assistant school principal should spend as much time with slow student learner programs as he or she does with talented student programs. ___T ___F

4. A teacher might have in his or her class a student that is a learning disabled/gifted student (the student's disability does not have to be physical). ___T ___F

5. Much research supports the benefits of heterogeneous grouping. ___T ___F

6. Due to the negative results of micro-managing, assistant school principals will best serve the school by not monitoring student achievement progress. ___T ___F

7. One of the problems of trying to implement accountability for the results of student performance is that there is no way that learning can be judged as a return on investment (ROI) as done in a business enterprise. ___T ___F

8. Learning-leader literature and empirical evidence commonly conclude that, first and foremost, the success of a learning-centered school depends largely on the administrators of the school. ___T ___F

9. In a learning-centered school, each student in the school is the responsibility of every teacher. ___T ___F

10. One of the problems often faced by learning-centered school efforts is having students "reach for more than what is thought possible." ___T ___F

Answers: 1–F, 2–F, 3–T, 4–T, 5–T, 6–T, 7–F, 8–T, 9–T, 10–F.
   Ratings:

10–9 correct   Skip the next section of the chapter; you know it already.

8–7 correct   Examine the next section of the chapter for the rationale given for the two or three answers that you missed.

6–5 correct   Read the next section rapidly.

4–3 correct   Read the next section and take notes.

2 or less correct   Enjoy the full reading of the next section and then retake the
 pre-section quiz.

Let's Consider the Rationale for the Answers to the Pre-Section Quiz

Statement 1 is false. Schools that have established and maintained a learning-centered school also have endorsed the adage that "failure is not an option." Learning at leisure or for leisure will not meet today's demands for highly knowledgeable and skilled workers. Individuals without the minimal education of a high school diploma today find themselves outside looking in. A high school education or special training in a vocational/technical school is required for almost every entry-level job. Student graduation is a top priority. We observed a school assistant principal conferring with a student who we will call Magell. Magell was 17 and a junior in high school. He was receiving failing grades in two subjects even though he had an IQ score of 115. He informed the assistant principal that he was dropping out of school and was getting his parents' to sign an approval for him to join the Navy. The assistant principal's conversation with Magell was brief. He said to Magell, "We cannot achieve our school's achievement goal unless you stay with us, contribute in every way that you can to our school's mission, and graduate from school next year." With some special academic support, Magell remained in school and graduated the following year.

Statement 2 is false. Parental involvement in their children's education has a significant effect on the level of achievement from the beginning to the end of the child's schooling. The research evidence is clear that when schools and parents support and encourage children's learning and development positive things happen. Student achievement is most positively affected when parents encourage a learning environment at home, hold high expectations for their child's achievement and are actively involved in their child's education both in the home and in the community (Henderson & Berla, 1994). It appears that parental involvement in education results in benefits for everyone: the children, parents, educators and the school. Empirical evidence indicates that the quality of parental involvement looms more important than the time they spend in such activities.

The levels of parental involvement in their child's education differ greatly. The school has to consider these differences and be prepared to "fill in" the involvement voids when they occur. Many schools nationally have homeless students. Single parents, working parents, and apathetic parents do exist. The need is clear. What the wisest and best parents want for their children, the school must provide for all children.

Statement 3 is true. We have emphasized throughout the book that monitoring, assessing, evaluating and changing school program activities are essential in a learning-centered school. Although we encourage pilot programs and learning interventions for the purpose of testing the potential of better program results, you cannot waste time on "good ideas" that just are not working. Every program plan should have a back-up plan that is set into operation so that students are not endangered academically. Ongoing assessment is one answer to this problem. Simply asking the students why learning is not happening to the extent that it should might point to needed changes in teaching methods and activities.

Statement 4 is true. Some students have a discrepant pattern of abilities whereby they have severe learning disabilities in one or more areas and show outstanding abilities in others (Norton et al., 1996). For example, an LD/G student might perform high levels of mathematical computations but have difficulty with reading and spelling skills. Landrum (1989) points out that these students have the ability to cover up or compensate for disabilities since disabilities and strengths tend to cancel each other out. Thus, LD/G students often are considered as average student achievers and their "true identities" in many instances go undiscovered and untreated.

Statement 5 is true. Heterogeneous grouping assumes different organizational plans. One arrangement simply places students of the same age group in one classroom regardless of their achievement levels. Multi-aged grouping or the non-graded primary school is also referred to as being heterogeneous since age differences are not the bases for class assignments, rather the student's achievement level is the primary determinant of subject placement. One of the primary purposes of the non-graded school is to eliminate the stigma of student failure. Supporters of non-graded school organizations argue that progress is measured in terms of the individual achievement of the student; continuous progress marks the status of each learner as opposed to failing or being promoted to the next higher grade.

Since heterogeneous grouping assumes several different organizational arrangements, research results on the topic become somewhat inconsistent. Thus, the answer to Statement #5 could be either true or false, depending on the actual grouping being addressed. Thus, give yourself credit for either answer given for #5.

Statement 6 is false. On the contrary, an ongoing plan of monitoring, assessing and evaluating student progress is essential. In one elementary school, the principal had the names of every child in the school on a grid that traced the academic progress of each one. Color-coded entries allowed the school principal to discern readily the lack of progress or slow progress of a learner. In those cases of little or no progress, a conference of appropriate school personnel took place at the earliest time possible to discuss the case and possible program interventions.

Teachers have reported the benefits of having students keep records and graphs of their own achievement in quiz/test results. In one case, target scores were set for learning objectives in reading. Reading speed and understanding results were recorded on a progress line graph indicating whether improvement had or had not been achieved and the extent to which the student had met or not met his/

her target objectives. Was it difficult for the teacher to track all of these activities? Not in the case at hand; pairs of students worked together to accomplish the task. For example, for speed-reading, one student would read and the partner served as the timer. Encourage your teachers to encourage their students to take a greater role in their own education.

Statement 7 is false. The business term, **return on investment (ROI)**, refers to the cost of establishing the business transaction and the returns received upon its implementation. For an educational investment in an in-service program for school personnel, the cost of programming the activity could be examined against the positive results attained by the program. For example, assume that the school spent $5,000 on an in-service activity for teachers that centered on the use of technology in the classroom for the purpose of improving student achievement in mathematics. An additional $10,000 was expended on the technological equipment. A pre-test was used to test the students' achievement levels before and after the in-service program was completed and a post-test was administered after the new program had been implemented and completed. The question to be answered centered on whether or not the difference between the pre- and post-test was significant. If little or no student gains in mathematics were realized, the ROI would be unsatisfactory. On the other hand, a significant difference would indicate that the return on investment was positive. You should look for hard data results in determining the value of program interventions and changes. In the foregoing example, a hard data statistic resulted. A report that 75 percent of the math teachers in the school district attended the in-service program would represent only soft data since it sheds no information about the results of its implementation on student achievement.

Statement 8 is true. It is difficult to find a study that does not support the importance of the school administrations' leadership for improving student academic performance and achieving a learning-centered school. In fact, a growing body of evidence supports the positive relationship between effective principal leadership and student learning and student achievement (Leithwood and Seashore-Louis, 2011). In the same vane, research has concluded that effects of leadership on student achievement are second only to classroom instruction in their contribution to student learning. We have emphasized throughout this book the paramount importance of your leadership in fostering teacher motivation that results in positive student achievement. You must work closely with the school principal and school staff in establishing a common vision and building cooperative teamwork that facilitates its accomplishment. Your leadership is showing when you stress the importance of the school's faculty and staff in reaching the goals and objectives of the school's mission.

When you do everything that you can to explain and demonstrate what it is that the school should accomplish, you will find that your school personnel are in a better position to help carry out what needs to be done. The key question is this: What is it that we are really trying to accomplish? The answer to this question is vested in your ability to define the goals and work with the staff to implement successful procedures.

Statement 9 is true. In our interviews with school principals and assistant principals, these administrators continually emphasized the importance of teamwork and faculty collaboration in terms of student advocacy. The status and needs of Johnny, a student in Miss Jones' sixth-grade class, become the concerns of all teachers in the school. The combined knowledge and expertise regarding the decisions for the matter at hand are utilized in helping Johnny improve. The assistant school principal commonly serves as the supervisor of support services that apply to needed interventions for Johnny's school program activities.

Suzanne Peterson (2014, May 4) believes that great leaders build teams by delegating. She notes that there are times to delegate and times when not to delegate. You should delegate when your workload is so full that you can't get your work done, when others can do the task just as well as you, when you need to provide growth experiences for others, and when you need time to grow yourself. One should not delegate when the person is not ready to assume the responsibility, or delegate and then change your mind later. Give credit to the person to whom you delegated the assignment.

No one has said it better than Pickett and Gerlach (2003), who defined **teamwork** as a process among partners who share mutual goals and work together to achieve the goals. They underscore the point that teamwork doesn't happen by accident. On the contrary, teamwork challenges one's ability to work cooperatively with others. It also challenges you to be able to create a cooperative relationship within the faculty and staff personnel. When accomplished, it enables the school faculty and staff to accept the hard work that goes along with teamwork. When teamwork succeeds it fosters growth and development on the part of the faculty and staff. Most importantly, teamwork results in positive benefits for students.

Assistant principals play an important role as supervisors and mentors in achieving teamwork. They contribute essential leadership for the team's success. We adapted Pickett and Gerlach's (2003) team characteristics for supervisors and mentors to the supervisory role of the assistant principal. Gerlach (2014) revealed the many ways in which supervisors and mentors can serve school teams (see Figure 4.1).

Statement 10 is false. High expectations for student achievement continue to be a positive goal of effective schools. However, the expectation must be for all students and not just the teacher's best learners. Empirical evidence makes it clear that teachers tend to expect that their slow learners will not achieve satisfactorily and their actions demonstrate this belief. That is, teachers tend to smile less in the presence of slow learners, call on them less and do not encourage more in-depth answers from them when called upon. The student sees this behavior and acts accordingly. One study concluded that just mentioning the high expectations and confidence of students in regard to a topic of study increased student achievement responses. Positive words that are supported by positive behaviors have positive effects on student performance.

Assistant Principal and the Teamwork Process

- Sets expectations of team member performance
- Offers challenging plans and ideas
- Helps build self-confidence of the team members
- Encourages ethical and professional behavior
- Offers support
- Actively listens
- Leads and teaches by example
- Provides growth experiences
- Asks questions and gives explanations
- Coaches the team members
- Encourages the team members
- Inspires the team members
- Shares critical knowledge
- Assists, observes and demonstrates effective practice
- Directs and delegates effectively
- Gives clear and concise directions

FIGURE 4.1 Characteristics of Supervisor and Mentors in the Teamwork Process

Source: Adapted from Kent Gerlach (2014, May 1). *Teamwork:Key to Success for Teachers and Paraeducators*. Impact Newsletter, University of Minnesota, Minneapolis. From the web: file:///Users/Scott/Desktop/Impact%20Newsletter:%20Teamwork:%20Key%20to%20Success%20for%20Teachers%and%and%29Paraeducators.webarchive

---

Snapshot 4.1—Flight 4923 Is On Parade

The story is told of an Air Force basic training group, Flight 4923. The basic training of the flight had experienced several problems. Its reputation of low standard performance in the classroom and on the field was frequent conversation. Each flight in the squadron was required to participate in the marching drill competition during basic training. As the day for the competition for Flight 4923 came to pass, the master sergeant in charge of basic training came to the barracks of the flight and said just loud enough for everyone to hear, "Well, we don't expect much from this flight in the drill competition today, but just don't embarrass us."

As Flight 4923 reached the location of the field where the competition was to be held, the flight's drill sergeant said to the seventy airmen in the flight, "I don't care what anyone else says, I have full confidence in you guys." You could just hear the steps of the airmen hit the pavement with a more even and rapid beat. Ten other flights competed in the drill exercises. The performance of Flight 4923 was given first place in the competition that day.

Learning Leadership: What Does Performance Evaluation Have to Do With It?

Performance assessment and evaluation require much more than a classroom observation. Box 4.1 sets forth the competency expectations for the school principal in relation to developing and implementing a performance improvement process.

Box 4.1 The Assistant Principal's Required Competencies for Teacher Performance Appraisal and Evaluation

Competencies

1.0 Ability to develop and implement a plan of performance evaluation for faculty personnel.

Indicator

1.1 Works with staff in identifying school goals and objectives related to establishing a learning culture in the school.

2.0 Ability to develop assessment procedures for determining improved teacher competency in classroom performance.

Indicators

2.1 Utilizes a variety of assessment strategies for assessing and evaluating teacher performance.

2.2 Involves teachers in the assessment and evaluation of performance.

Views formative evaluation as a self-development process.

3.0 Ability to communicate effectively with school personnel in the performance evaluation process.

Indicators

3.1 Establishes schedules for performance assessments that include pre-conferences, the classroom observation, observation feedback, and post-observation conference.

3.2 Communicates effectively with personnel concerning outstanding achievements and contributions.

3.3 Communicates effectively with personnel regarding improvement needs. Works with the teacher in designing an individual improvement plan.

4.0 Ability to collect and synthesize performance data from all areas included in the performance assessment.

Indicators

4.1 Interprets assessment data in terms of the school's goals and objectives.

4.2 Emphasizes performance strengths and confers with the teacher relative to how the strengths can be extended in his or her teaching.

5.0 Ability to facilitate staff growth and development through the creation of a variety of program activities and opportunities.

Indicators

5.1 Supports the teacher's recommendations for follow-up strategies for achieving performance growth related to personal strengths and identified improvement needs.

5.2 Gives needed attention to providing the time required for growth and development activities.

Assessing Classroom Teaching and Student Data: Identifying Program Strengths and Improvement Needs

Perhaps you have had little or no experience using data toward the objective of improving student academic performance. The role of an assistant principal as a learning leader definitely will require you to be highly competent in data collection and in data analysis and evaluation. In the following section, we provide certain guidelines for improving your own competency in using data to make better decisions about program provisions and instructional strategies.

Due to the contemporary emphasis on student academic performance, teacher performance assessment instruments are primarily designed to measure the classroom performance as it demonstrates this dimension. We agree with this point of emphasis, but contend that the quality teacher demonstrates additional traits in professional areas of importance. Each of the performance areas shown in Box 4.2 looms important relative to important aspects of effective schools. In addition, each area in the box lends significantly to the effectiveness of classroom teaching.

Box 4.2 Areas of Teacher Performance

Areas of Teacher Performance for Assessment and Evaluation

1. Scholarship

a. Preparation

   (1) Communication Skills (ability to use appropriate written and oral communication skills)

   (2) Specific Knowledge (ability to accurately quantify and organize subject-matter; familiarity with sources of instructional materials; ability to implement the school's course of study)

   (3) General Scholarship (breadth of information and experience and ability to apply this knowledge in practice)

   (4) Professional Knowledge (ability to acquire and apply knowledge of contemporary theory and practices; knowledge and use of educational psychology)

b. Evidence of Professional Growth

   (1) Record of professional growth and development activities and hard data evidence of its results (ability to meet the school board's policy requirements relative to professional development)

2. Teaching Performance

a. Ability to plan and organize for effective teaching

   (1) Definitive goals and objectives for student learning

   (2) Adapts to students' needs, interests and capacity

   (3) Uses appropriate learning materials and aids to enhance student learning

   (4) Teaches according to the curriculum guides planned and approved by the school and school district

b. Ability to demonstrate resourcefulness in carrying out the responsibilities of the position description

   (1) Uses strategies to identify students' learning styles and uses teaching methods to accommodate the respective styles in the best way possible

   (2) Works effectively in inclusive classrooms

c. Ability to implement resourcefulness in relation to student learning

   (1) Develops strategies to set the stage for student learning

   (2) Uses a variety of teaching methods and aids to facilitate student learning

(3) Collects appropriate data as related to student achievement progress

(4) Gives equal attention and respect to all students in regard to learning needs and participation in learning activities

d. Ability to collect and assess student-learning outcomes

(1) Compares student achievement outcome data with course/student expectations

(2) Uses a variety of formal and informal assessment measures to determine the student's learning success level

(3) Makes changes and/or interventions as appropriate for improved student learning

3. Personal and Professional Management

a. Ability to foster a positive learning climate in the classroom

(1) Discusses the expectations of personal behavior with students and implements positive discipline measures in cases of behavior violations

b. Ability to maintain a positive relationship with students and show each student his or her personal respect

4. Professional Attitude and Demeanor

a. Ability to work cooperatively with co-workers and show pride in the school and education profession

b. Ability to contribute to the school's goals and objectives in various ways and respect decisions made by the consensus of the staff

c. Ability to participate and contribute to the professional groups and associations of choice

d. Ability to contribute to the fostering of a positive school learning climate in the school

e. Ability to work cooperatively with a sense of respect and open-mindedness with faculty personnel, students, parents and other members of the school community.

What Important Student Data Must Be Collected and Assessed?

Previously we stated that learning target objectives should be measurable. Major assessment instruments should be ones that have been tested for validity and reliability. Tests with both state and national norms serve a good purpose. These test provisions are beneficial in completing activities related to data analysis.

Data analysis essentially is the process of closely examining the collection of data required by your improvement plan and reading the "tea leaves." What do the data tell you about the current status of student learning? What academic areas reveal positive signs of improvement? What data areas make it clear that improvements are needed and/or the present learning strategies in that area are not being successful? If one program area has been unsuccessful, were there events during the school year that might have influenced the results negatively? What practices were good and which ones were not effective? What improvement priorities were evident? What special program strengths do the data reveal and how can these strengths be extended in our school programs? What learning patterns seem to jump up to be recognized? Does it seem clear that our teamwork collaboration has had an important effect on what we do for students?

Well, that seems to take care of it. Not quite yet. Now we use our leadership and the motivation from our previous progress to move ahead. Our improvement team(s) gets back to work. It reviews the priority needs and begins to focus on goals for the forthcoming year and the years ahead.

The Assistant Principal's Need to Become a Quality Teacher Performance Evaluator

Most states have quality performance appraisal in-service programs. If so, you most likely could skip this last section of the chapter. If you do not hold a quality performance evaluation certificate, you could take the following brief quiz to "test" your knowledge of teacher performance evaluation.

Quiz on Teacher Performance Appraisal

Directions: Check your answer of true or false to each of the following performance appraisal questions.

1. A formative performance evaluation is administered at specified times to provide data and information relative to continuation of employment, tenure, or employee dismissal. ___T ___F

2. The knowledge and skill criteria for a qualified evaluator center exclusively on one dimension, that of the classroom observation. ___T ___F

3. The basic categories of performance appraisal systems are integral, relational and collaborative. ___T ___F

4. Both empirical and basic research have determined that the best time to assess a teacher's classroom performance is at the end of the first semester or the end of the second semester when he or she has had ample time to provide optimal student learning. ___T ___F

5. A performance evaluation that centers on professional development purposes is termed a formal evaluation. ____T ____F

The foregoing statements are among those that we discuss in the following section. In the quiz, Statement 1 is F, 2 is F, 3 is F, 4 is F and 5 is F. The following section centers on the primary purposes of performance appraisal. In addition, we consider the appraisal process and the need for strict adherence to school board and state policies, the classroom observations, walkthrough evaluations, and the components of a quality evaluator's in-service workshop. It is common that the assistant principal and principal share responsibility for performance assessments. However, assistant principals usually participate in formative assessment while the principal assumes the primary responsibility for summative performance assessments.

The Formative Performance Evaluation: Toward the Goal of Improved Instruction

Almost all school principals would agree that state and school board requirements related to teacher performance assessments take up at least 25 percent of their time. Performance assessments require much more than classroom observations. Especially for formative performance evaluations, pre-assessment sessions are necessary as well as post-assessment conferences, and follow-up improvement feedback must be accomplished. It comes down to the fact that assistant principals will need to be highly qualified performance evaluators or they will not be effective in that administrative role today.

A **formative evaluation** has the primary purpose of improving the teacher's classroom performance for student learning. Thus, the teacher participates in all phases of the evaluation activity including the planning of the observation, determining the lesson goals and objectives, identifying the instructional strategies to be used and describing the student participation to be implemented. What? No surprise observations? Can't the teacher just put on an act and then go back to his or her regular ways of teaching? If such a practice is in place, then the objective of instructional improvement is flawed. High performing teachers view personal growth and development as self-development. We submit that professional teachers welcome classroom visitations. Most commonly, they ask administrative personnel and other teachers to observe them and provide feedback. They use self-evaluation strategies continuously. When this attitude occurs throughout the staff, the characteristics of a learning school culture are in evidence.

The most common type of performance appraisal system used in education is termed **rating system**. Rating systems use various criteria such as job competencies, state and/or school board standards, and role responsibilities to judge knowledge and skill levels (Young, 2008). A number system rating scale serves to differentiate the level of performance of each entry. For example, a rating scale of 5–high to 1–low or 5–behavior always in evidence to 1–behavior not in evidence is used to differentiate knowledge and skill levels. A **ranking system** is competitive in the sense that assessment results are compared with other employees in the same job family. This system is used commonly for ranking jobs of classified workers. The ranking method ranks jobs from highest to lowest in terms of value to the organization. The system ties closely to the process of job grading that is used primarily for salary allocation purposes. For example, job levels could range from executive to skilled worker to semi-skilled worker to unskilled worker. Another closely related system is the **factor comparison method**. This method ranks factors such as mental effort, physical effort, skill level needed, responsibility level, accountability level, supervision requirements, working conditions and problem solving responsibilities. The factors for evaluation most often are determined as a result of a job analysis that serves to identify them.

A **narrative system** focuses on the position's required tasks and competencies. In some instances the employee's work products are examined as part of the evaluation. A job record or portfolio commonly is used to provide an analysis of the job purposes, employee's work objectives, methods and outcomes. In the case of classified workers, examples of work products and/or actual work performances "on the spot" might be utilized to assess the employee.

Formative performance evaluations differ from summative evaluations both in terms of their purposes and their outcomes. As discussed, formative teacher performance assessments center on improvement motives; improvement of instruction leads to improvement of student learning.

A **summative performance evaluation** is administered for such purposes as employee retention, tenure status, employee performance pay, and placement on the school system's salary tracks. In almost all cases, the school principal administers summative teacher evaluations. However, state laws most often state that the local school board shall designate persons who are qualified to evaluate teachers to serve as evaluators for the district's teacher performance evaluation system. State laws and school board policies commonly determine the regulations for completing summative evaluations. Most state laws have regulations that focus on the school board's primary responsibility for establishing a system for performance evaluation, setting specific procedures for administering the evaluations of employees, indicating the specific performance times for evaluations, the need for qualified persons to administer the evaluations, describing the nature of the evaluation report, stating how the report is to be disseminated, establishing the need to include improvement recommendations in the report, emphasizing the nature of privacy in handling the evaluation results, and stating the possible uses of the evaluation report including its possible use in court action or official hearings.

The Classroom Observation and Utilization of the Classroom Walk-Through

Classroom observation requirements, according to school principals, change often and in some cases year to year. The classroom walk-through evaluation is gaining increased use since it permits the evaluator to visit more classrooms more often. In many cases, the evaluator might not need to be in a classroom for more than ten minutes to observe a specified teacher behavior that has been cited for improvement. For example, if a previous classroom observation had noted that the teaching lesson objectives had not been stated or that classroom behavior standards were not displayed, a walk-through observation might focus only on these two criteria. One principal kept a running record of the last time that she had visited the classroom of every teacher in the school. In this way she was able to check the last time any one teacher had been visited and to schedule future visits accordingly.

A **walk-through classroom evaluation** form commonly includes one sheet of five or more primary instructional criteria. For example, the criterion of teaching objective(s), introductory set, instructional materials and aids, teaching methods, student participation, and classroom environment are common listings. A simple yes or no check is used to indicate the observation status of entries under these major criteria headings. Included on the sheet is a section for written comments that remind the observer of the specific purposes of the walk-through and the particular strengths and/or needs that were observed by the teacher.

The Classroom Observation

As previously noted, state laws and school board policies typically set forth the regulations relating to the frequency of teacher performance evaluations. A common practice is to have two performance evaluations each year for non-tenured teacher personnel and one for tenured personnel. Three classroom observations for non-tenured teachers have certain advantages. The first evaluation could be administered at the very outset of a new instructional unit when the unit is being introduced, unit objectives are being discussed and ties to the previous lesson are being made. The second observation could be scheduled near the middle of the unit when student activities are underway and the teacher's instructional methods and strategies can be readily observed and student engagement in learning can be observed. The third observation provides an opportunity to witness the closing of the unit lesson and the extent to which the unit objectives have been achieved.

An appropriate post-observation conference should follow each classroom observation. In the case of a formative evaluation the teacher's strengths are stressed, including ways in which these strengths might be extended in his or her teaching. As has been stated by Clifton and Nelson (1992), teachers soar with their strengths. It isn't that the teacher's needs or weaknesses should not be considered, rather the emphasis should not be placed on remediation. The outcomes of exercising one's strong competencies will result in far more positive learning outcomes for students.

The topic of personnel growth and development is discussed further in Chapter 5.

Staff Growth and Development: Schools Progress as their People Grow and Develop

Implementing the Improvement Process

When the school team begin their thinking about improving student learning, they must first agree on what it is that they want to improve. You want to improve learning, but what objectives do you want to achieve? The targets that you want to meet can be established for both a certain class/group or for individual students. Are the targets focused on results for academic learning or perhaps for other purposes such as student attendance, reduction of dropout rates, school climate improvement or student civic responsibilities? In any case, improvement targets must be stated clearly and in measurable terms. For example, two such improvement target statements are as follows:

- To improve student behavior so that student "office visits" for behavior violations are reduced by 75 percent by the end of the forthcoming school year.

- To improve the reading scores of students in all elementary school grades so that 80 percent of students are reading at or above the reading proficiency level by the end of grade 6 according to the state's reading proficiency standards.

In regard to the first example relating to student behavior, what hard data, besides the number of students sent to the office at the end of the forthcoming year, might be appropriate to assess this target objective? For example, what surveys might be beneficial to assess target results? In relation to the second target statement, assessments of student reading achievement in each grade should be administered periodically at every grade level. Results from these assessments could point toward needed program interventions long before the grade 6 state proficiency test is administered.

Once target objectives are completed steps must be taken to implement the improvement plan. Time should be made available for improvement teams to bring themselves up to date on pertinent research, best practices, student learning styles and other recent literature that pertains to implementation methods and strategies.

One school found that time for such discussion was gained when they changed their regular faculty meetings to program improvement sessions. Information that previously had been disseminated in faculty meetings was sent and digested successfully via a short faculty "news page." In any case, target dates and work completion are things that the assistant school principal must keep in mind through periodic checks of progress and recording progress data on charts for all to examine.

Improvement teams have found the giving of specific assignments to a member or members of the improvement team to be successful. Who is going to be responsible for what? Some assignments are short-term and others might take a few weeks. In any case, members report back their findings/conclusions for all team members to consider.

Empirical evidence suggests that the best personal growth and development takes place through the individual team member assignments and the follow-up discussions. How will the success of our interventions and program activities be assessed? How will individual class assessments be handled? What external tests will be administered and by whom?

The Concept of Professional Growth as Self-Development

A primary competency requirement of the assistant principal is the ability to organize and conduct growth activities for certificated and classified personnel. Related indicators of this competency are: (1) develops and administers meaningful in-service programs, (2) shares appropriate articles and monographs for the staff, (3) suggests appropriate continuing education, and (4) encourages research for practical use. Each of these indicators of competency is discussed in the following sections of the chapter.

The Assistant Principal's Leadership Role in Developing and Administering Meaningful In-Service Programs

We take the position that the most effective **staff development** is self-development. The concept of self-development centers on the practice of having the individual employee assume a major role in the assessment, analysis and implementation of his or her improvement activities. This is not to imply that other persons do not take part or support the individual's staff development program, rather the individual assumes the primary responsibility relative to determining the goals and objectives of the development program to be pursued. A coach or mentor commonly helps the individual assess his or her strengths and needs, but the individual uses personal initiative in designing their own learning activities. Such an approach to development contends that individuals are highly motivated by having the freedom to choose the design of their own learning. This point is supported by Rogers (1969) in his early statement that learning has to be self-discovered and self-appropriated if it is to have significant influences on one's behavior.

In any case, self-development cannot be a casual and periodic activity that the individual decides to partake. Rather, a conscious effort must be made to assess one's development need(s), to set forth a plan that provides meaningful opportunities to meet the needs, to investigate the most appropriate activities for implementing the plan, to schedule and participate in the activities, and to use objective measures to "test" the effectiveness of the plan. Several questions need your attention. What hard evidence is available to support the current status of my personal improvement? What are strengths that I can extend in my teaching practice? What areas should be given priority in terms of needed improvement? What activities will best serve my performance improvement? What was the ROI of my time and effort in relation to the improvement gains?

As you work with your teachers, your responsibilities as assistant principal center on serving as a mentor and supervisor. Your primary service as a mentor is that of listening. You listen and allow the mentee to think through the viability of his or her self-development plan. Is the improvement plan well conceived? What went well in the implementation plan and why? Is the plan worthy of continuation? What did not go as well as expected and why? You allow the individual to reach his or her own conclusions. If asked, you respond, but mentors commonly answer questions with a question.

The possibilities for pursuing self-development activities are almost endless. Such activities for the teacher might include taking a class or attending a special workshop, examining the research on a topic related to the teacher's interests and needs, pursuing activities in a teacher center in the school district or within the community, writing a mini-grant proposal, doing research and writing an article for possible publication on a topic of interest, scheduling a number of visitations to the classrooms of other district teachers that reportedly have similar interests to their own, and others that serve the purposes of the teacher's development goals and objectives.

The Classroom and Walk-Through Observation: Follow-Up Development Practices

In some cases, the follow-up of a walk-through observation might be a simple note to the teacher in his or her mailbox or a brief feedback comment delivered in person. If, for example, a previous classroom observation report for a math teacher had noted the need to improve the introduction or setting of a unit, you might comment as follows:

> Your introduction to the unit on quadratic equations was excellent. You tied the topic to the students' previous work on linear equations, pointed

out briefly the different ways that quadratic equations might be solved, alluded to the differences between linear and quadratic equations in graphing, underscored the applications of quadratics, and outlined what the students were expected to learn in the unit, and opened that day's lesson by defining the term, quadratic equation and illustrating its standard form, $ax^2 + bx + c = 0$. I noted that you completed the set of the unit in six minutes. Nice job.

In many instances, a positive comment serves a good purpose. "Sara, with your initiative, you can complete most anything that you choose to do." "Rita, may I borrow some of your positive outlook? You always are able to see the bright side of things." "Manuel, you are what is called a teacher's teacher. You certainly are a teacher-leader." "Merlin, if everyone had your technology talent, we would have to change the name of our school to Whittier Technical Learning Center." Such genuine comments often initiate corresponding positive behaviors.

It seems clear that the primary objective of feedback sessions is to provide the teacher with specific information and data that can be considered and potentially implemented for improving the teacher's classroom performance and result in improved student learning. However, just telling the teacher about a need for improvement does not automatically result in its implementation in practice. We will emphasize the use of a clinical approach to illustrate a feedback strategy that is direct, purposeful, continuous and empirically validated in practice.

Improving Teacher Performance Through the Process of Clinical Supervision

Goldhammer (1969) reportedly introduced the process of clinical supervision into education more than forty-five years ago. The process evolved from the medical profession that historically used the process for developing the medical competencies required in practice. Norton (2008) noted that **clinical supervision** in education serves the school system by improving instruction through improving staff performance. We view staff development in relation to the concept of self-development. Although the assistant principal or other qualified performance evaluator assists in a supportive role, the teacher assumes the primary responsibility of evaluating his or her own performance and implementing appropriate improvements.

We subscribe to the process of clinical supervision since it sets forth specific competencies on the part of the school administrator to implement with the specific purpose of improving student achievement in the school. The process commonly consists of four primary phases that include various steps within the improvement cycle.

The Clinical Supervision's Cyclical Process

1. **The initial pre-observation conference**. The cooperative relationship between the teacher and the assistant principal is established. The nature of the clinical supervision process is discussed and the ways in which the assistant principal will support the process are discussed. The expectations for the teacher are clarified and the essentials of this formative process are reviewed. The follow-up procedures are discussed and questions on the part of the teacher are answered. The teacher selects an instructional unit for the classroom observation with the cooperation of the administrator. Instructional objectives, teaching strategies, teaching materials, student participation and related learning activities are discussed. The focus of the initial pre-observation is that of planning the observation procedures, including the nature of the learners in the classroom and any conditions that require special attention. For example, will the classroom observation be taped? If agreed upon, how will the technical requirements be installed in the classroom?

2. **The Assistant Principal Completes the Classroom Observation**. The classroom observation is completed by the assistant principal using the methods agreed upon in the pre-observation conference. The assistant principal uses the appropriate observation assessment form that in some cases is required by the state and/or by the local school board. Following the observation the teacher and assistant principal review the collected data and discuss any necessary clarifications. The assistant principal organizes the data into a meaningful report for use in the post-conference. The assistant principal plans the post-observation conference using the format agreed upon in the pre-conference and checks with the teacher on post-observation matters as needed. It is not uncommon for the teacher to work directly with the assistant principal if that arrangement is the preference of the teacher.

3. **Implementation of the Post-Observation Conference**. The post-observation conference is an essential step in the improvement process. Trust has been developed between the two participants and an opportunity to review and evaluate the observation data in relation to the pre-determined class objectives is provided. The assistant principal's role at this time is that of teacher and mentor. The major focus is on the data at hand and what it reveals in terms of the teacher's strengths and behavior changes that might be needed for follow-up classroom performances.

4. **Planning the Next Teaching Lesson**. The final step in the cycle is the planning of the future teaching lesson(s). The identified changes in the teacher's methods and classroom behaviors are adapted into the improvement

plan for future lessons. The improvement relationships between the teacher and assistant principal continue and the efforts of both parties are re-focused on step 1 of the clinical supervision cycle.

The Assistant Principal Suggests a Program of Continuing Education for All School Personnel

Supporting your faculty in the designing of their own individual development plan (IDP) will lead to positive learning results. Improvement plans commonly are generated following the implementation of a performance observation. In doing so, it is important that you give your best teachers equal time. Empirical evidence suggests that administrative support is one of the primary factors that serve to retain teachers in your school. Individual development programs commonly are detailed plans for active involvement in improvement programs and activities. Positive support might be no more than helping the teacher stay with the improvement plan. An improvement plan is just a plan until it is implemented and carried out.

A personal development plan often is viewed as a requirement for a marginal employee to pursue. We view such a plan as being advantageous for all employees. Effective plans tend to focus on one's strengths as opposed to weakness. As mentioned throughout this book, people tend to soar with their strengths (Clifton and Nelson, 1992). An effective improvement plan fosters the concept of self-development. The teacher is mainly the one in charge of his or her life. Improvement is more likely to happen when the person understands what it is that he or she wants to accomplish. Development is not something that the teacher does next week or even next year. On the contrary, development looks forward to the teacher's future. We understand, of course, that a marginal teacher's improvement needs most likely will require a more immediate timeline, but improvement generally requires meaningful support and time to accomplish the desired ends.

Snapshot 4.2—Support Plus Courage = Positive Results

In one case, a competent middle school first-year teacher had a speaking style that was difficult for students to understand. Part of the problem was that she had what is often termed a distinct Southern accent with a rapid speech pattern. Parents complained vocally about the problem, and since one of the teacher's parents was a member of the school board, the problem received immediate attention. The superintendent was being pressured to move on this matter. He asked the school principal to initiate actions that would assess the teacher's performance. The principal delegated the task to the school's assistant principal.

In brief, the assistant principal conferred with the teacher, gained some rapport, and suggested that part of the teacher's lesson be recorded. Both the teacher and the assistant principal listened to the recording. Upon its completion, the teacher remarked, "Do I really talk like that?" Although the assistant principal was not a speech therapist, he worked with the teacher on slowing her speech and improving her pronunciation. The problem was significantly resolved. Although there continued to be some resentment about the teacher, her teaching skills were most satisfactory and her speech was satisfactory as well. At a special meeting, the school superintendent recommended a dismissal hearing for the teacher. The assistant principal responded, "If a hearing is scheduled on this case, I will have to state that the teacher has demonstrated significant improvement and is performing satisfactorily in the classroom at this time." That prevented any further action in this case.

Teachers as Adult Learners

The effective assistant principal is a consumer, disseminator and implementer of valid and reliable research. Successful staff development programs in education display several common features. One such feature is that attention has been given to adult learning research and these principles are implemented in the program's activities. Knowles and associates (1984) point out the differences between **pedagogy and andragogy**. Pedagogy centers on the principles of teaching children and andragogy on the principles of teaching adults. In regard to adult learning, adults want to know that the learning will be such that it can be applied to practice. The concept commonly is viewed as being job-embedded. Will the learning experiences of the staff development experience help to enrich the learning of students? Will the experience lead to the resolution of problems faced in teaching the subject(s) at hand?

As adults, teachers want to be meaningfully involved in decisions relative to the staff development experiences. The activities have to be related to the teachers' interests and needs. What are the goals and objectives of the staff development program activities? Are the goals and objectives in direct relation to the teacher's individual development plan?

Successful development programs make certain that the "learners" will be actively involved in the learning process. Hands-on activities are much preferred to lectures or oral presentations. Teacher participants want to witness tangible evidence of their achievement resulting from the development experience. The experience has to add measurably to the teacher's expertise in the topic at hand. Emphasis on mere tips and/or strategies is to be avoided. Emphasis is placed on how the teacher can make the new learning lead to improvement in their personal classroom performance and improved student academic achievement. The assistant school principal has the challenge of supporting teachers' learning and helping them find ways to try out the learning concepts in their classrooms.

As noted by Stella Cottrell (2014) in her book *Skills for Success*, the advantages of taking a personal approach to growth and development are many. She cites the following advantages: (1) gaining a clearer focus to your learning, (2) helping to keep yourself motivated, (3) a better understanding of how you learn and how to improve your performance, (4) more enjoyment and less stress from your learning as you become consciously skilled, (5) more awareness of how you apply your learning to new problems and contexts, and (6) reflective thinking that can strengthen academic performance (p. 2).

Time must be available for teachers to meet and compare their successes in implementing new procedures and concepts. Without the assistant principal's leadership in assuring time for teacher collaboration, the staff development is likely to be flawed. Successful schools have used a variety of ways to gain time for teacher collaboration. One school in Arizona excused students from school for half a day each month on a Friday for staff development purposes. A principal in one school arranged the class schedules of teachers so that similar times for planning were available for some teachers. Several school principals noted that the regular faculty meetings of the school staff had been changed to program improvement sessions. Another school scheduled what was considered as "expert for teacher days" whereby local community and college/university personnel brought their expertise to the classroom while the teacher was involved in a staff development activity. The use of substitute teachers was also found to be an effective way to release the regular classroom teachers for collaborative staff development activity experiences.

One of the most effective, self-directed staff development activities comes under the title of "Individually Guided Staff Development." In this approach, identified in an article by the National Academy of Sciences (1990),

> the teachers, individually or in collegial teams, identify their interests and concerns; establish a goal; and seek input by way of coursework, workshops, library research, field trips, and other forms of self-study to reach the goal . . . Such an approach to staff development can complement, and in some cases replace, the traditional in-service workshop.

Get Ahead of the Question—What Was the Return on Investment for the School's Staff Development Program?

You will be ahead of the game if your school's staff development plan includes an evaluation component that results in some hard data evidence. Nevertheless, state legislators and school boards are asking whether monies being spent on professional conferences, teacher workshops, teacher centers, consultant services and other in-service activities might be better spent elsewhere. Once again, results that center on soft data such as the number in attendance at a professional workshop, the positive comments of participants regarding the effectiveness of the program, or the extent of the participants' enjoyment of the in-service experience do not meet the ROI requirements. Even evidence relative to the extent the "new knowledge" was implemented in the classroom will not be completely satisfactory.

The bottom line, of course, and the question that you must answer, is "What was the effect of the implementation of the new knowledge on student learning?" This question is not always easily answered or related data readily obtained.

Nevertheless, Guskey (2002, March), points out that "the bottom line" is how the professional development activity affected students. For example, the use of a comparison test, whereby the performance scores of students who used the "new student learning" were compared to the performance scores of those similar students who did not, does represent efforts to secure hard data information.

Guskey underscores other resultant information of importance in the evaluation of staff development program. Besides academic achievement data that center on cognitive performance, the outcomes relating to student attitudes and dispositions as well as skills and behaviors loom important in the students' growth and development. We submit that much more attention in our schools should be given to the affective, interpersonal, and psychomotor learning domains. Unfortunately, the cognitive domain related to performance in reading, math, English and science is the one that gains almost all the attention of state education offices and school boards.

Summary

The primary goal of Chapter 4 centered on defining the role of the assistant principal as a learning leader and bringing the role to the front line of the school's primary purposes. We suggested that placing the assistant principal at the center of the school's efforts to become a learning-centered school would bring "new life" to this administrative position.

If instruction is to be such that all students learn and improve academically, it must give full attention to the student's learning style. If, indeed, schools are to become learning-centered schools, the matter of how students learn must be studied, determined and implemented in practice.

Student interests and needs include the matter of setting high expectations for their learning. The chapter presented various strategies for helping students set challenging goals for learning and then achieving them. The research and empirical evidence on organizing an inclusive school was given emphasis. Inclusiveness benefits all students. Teamwork was recommended as a prerequisite for achieving an inclusive school. Achieving quality teamwork in schools depends largely on the school's administrative leaders. Student advocate leaders stick to their guns in leading the school toward inclusiveness that extends to all students.

The importance of collecting pertinent achievement data and analyzing what those data reveal is a competency of importance for any assistant principal. Once school leaders have helped each teacher understand the importance of collecting learning data and knowing ways to use it in improving student academic performance, a learning culture soon emerges and develops within the school. It is clear that effectiveness in the role requires all assistant principals to be highly competent in the processes of data collection, data analysis and data application for the primary purpose of improving student academic performance.

The chapter ended with a discussion of teacher professional growth and development. Personnel assessment and evaluation activities are of limited value unless they result in follow-up programs of faculty and staff growth and development.

Discussion Questions

1. Review the specific purposes of formative and summative evaluations. Should the same person serve as the performance evaluator for a particular employee? Why or why not? Present the reasons for your opinion.

2. The chapter submits that the assistant principal's positive effectiveness in the role of a learning leader will lend to the authenticity of the position. What does this contention mean to you?

3. The chapter gave considerable attention to the topic of student learning styles. To what extent do you believe that this concept is actually evident in practice? Note evidence of practice that you have witnessed regarding the identification of student learning styles and adjusting teaching methods and strategies.

CASE STUDIES

Case 4.1 A Case of Teacher Retention

Maria Lopez is an ELL teacher at Hawthorne Elementary School. The school's organizational plan has Maria scheduled to work with half of "her" ELL students in the morning and the other half in the afternoon. Her performance ratings have been highly satisfactory. Students that are in her classes in the morning attend subject-matter classes in the afternoon and the afternoon ELL students attend subject-matter classes in the morning. In this arrangement, Maria has had few opportunities to work with the subject-matter teachers in planning teaching strategies and instructional aids for the ELL students. Maria does attempt to visit with those teachers who have the same planning period as she, but visitations are spasmodic and she feels that the teachers are not really following through with her recommendations for the ELL students in their classrooms.

She stated that she does have the support of the school principal but that's about as far as it goes. The primary directions that Maria has been able to give to the classroom teachers is the two-hour in-service program time during planning week before the beginning of the school year.

Maria's frustration has caused her to come to the conclusion that this year will be her last year as an ELL teacher at Hawthorne. Although her professional interests still are positive in working with ELL students, she thinks that she could settle for returning to her previous position as a third-grade teacher and reading specialist in another school district.

Questions

1. Your task is to serve as the assistant school principal at Hawthorne Elementary School and retain Maria's services in the school for next year if at all possible. You do not have a magic wand to resolve present concerns or a large sum of dollars available in the school safe. With the limited information stated in the case study, set forth administrative actions that you would take in order to retain Maria's services.
2. In view of the major topics presented in Chapter 4, which topic or topics appear to be relevant to case 4.1?

References

Ask.com (April 26, 2014). *What is the definition of cognitive learning?* From the web: www.ask.com/question/what-is-the-definition-of-cognitive-learning.

Bloss, J.M. (1882). *Thirteenth report of the superintendent of public instruction of the state of Indiana to the governor.* Indianapolis: State of Indiana.

Church, A.H., & Bracken, D.W. (Eds.) (1997). Special issue: 360-degree feedback systems. *Group and Organization Management,* 22(2).

Clifton, D.O., & Nelson, P. (1992). *Soar with your strengths.* New York: Dell.

Cottrell, S. (2014). *Skills for success: Personal development and employability.* London and New York: Palgrave.

Falvey, M.A., & Givner, C.C. (2005). What is an inclusive school? Chapter 1 in *Creating an Inclusive School*, 2nd ed. Edited by Richard A. Villa and Jacqueline S. Thousand. Alexandria, VA: ASCD.

Fleming, N. (2001–2011). *VARK: A guide to learning styles*. Christchurch, New Zealand: Author.

Gerlach, K. (2014, May). Teamwork: Key to success for teachers and paraeducators. *Impact Newsletter*. From the web: file:///Users/Scott/Desktop/Impact%20Newsletter:%20Teamwork:%20Key%20to%20Success%20for%20Teachers%20and%20Paraeducators.webarchive

Goldhammer, R. (1969). *Clinical supervision*. New York: Holt, Rinehart & Winston.

Gregorc, A. (2011). *Mind styles*. Retrieved from the web, November 13, 2011. http://web.cortland.edu/andersmd/learning/Gregorc.htm

Guskey, T.R. (2002, March). Redesigning professional development: Does it make a difference? *Educational Leadership*, 59(6), 45–51.

Henderson, A.T., & Berla, N. (Eds.) (1994). *A new generation of evidence: The family is critical to student achievement*. Report from the National Committee for Citizens in Education. Washington, D.C.: Center for Law and Education.

Keefe, J.W. (2005, Spring). Assessment of learning style variables: The NASSP model. *Theory Into Practice. Learning and the Brain*, 24(2), 138–144. New York: Taylor & Francis.

Knowles, M., & Associates (1984). *Andragogy in action: Applying modern principles of adult learning*. San Francisco, CA: Jossey-Bass.

Kolb, D. (1984). *Experiential learning: Experience as the source of learning and development*. Englewood Cliffs, NJ: Prentice-Hall.

Landrum, T.J. (1989). Gifted and learning disabled students: Practical considerations for teachers. *Academic Therapy,* 24(5), 533–543.

Leithwood, K., & Seashore-Louis, K. (2011, December). *Linking leadership to student learning*. San Francisco, CA: Jossey Bass.

Lester, J.H. (2003). Planning effective secondary professional development programs. *American Secondary Education*, 32(1), 49–61.

Manatt, R.P., & Benway, M. (1998). Teacher and administrator performance: Benefits of 360-degree feedback. *ERS Spectrum*, 16(2), 18–23.

Marzano, R.J. (2010, September). Art and science teaching: High expectations for all. *EL Educational Leadership*, 10(1), 82–84.

Montgomery County Public Schools (1995–2014). *Preface to descriptive examples for assistant principals (and others) of school-based programs*. Rockville, MD: Department of Financial Services.

National Academy of Sciences (1990). Choose effective approaches to staff development. From chapter 12 of *Elementary school science for the 90's* by Susan Loucks-Horsley and Roxanne Kapitan. Alexandria, VA: ASCD.

National Council of Teachers of English (2014). On reading: Learning to read, and effective reading, what we know and how we know it. *NCTE Guideline*. Urbana, IL: Author.

National Research Council (1997). *Preparing for the 21st century: The education imperative*. Office of Congressional Government Affairs. Washington, D.C.: Government Printer.

Norton, M.S. (2008). *Human resources administration for educational leaders.* Thousand Oaks, CA: Sage.

Norton, M.S., Hunnicutt, K., & Norton, R.C. (1996). The learning disabled/gifted student. *Contemporary Education,* 67(1), 36–40.

Norton, M.S., Kelly, L.K., and Battle, A.R. (2012). *The principal as student advocate: A guide for doing what's best for all students.* Larchmont, NY: Eye on Education.

Ouchi, W. (1981). *Theory Z: How American business can meet the Japanese challenge.* Reading, MA: Addison-Wesley.

Pashler, H., McDaniel, M., Rohrer, D., & Bjork, R. (2008). Learning styles: Concepts and evidence. *Psychological Science in the Public Interest,* 9, 105–119.

Peterson, S. (2014, May 4). Great leaders build teams by delegating. *Career Builder, AZ Jobs.* Phoenix, AZ: Arizona Republic, p. E6.

Pickett, A.L., & Gerlach, K. (2003). *Supervising paraeducators in educational settings: A team approach.* 2nd ed. Austin, TX: Pro-ed.

Rogers, C.R. (1969). Freedom to learn (essay). From *Freedom to Learn.* Upper Saddle River, NJ: Merrill Publishing Company.

Shepard, L.A., & Smith, M.L. (Eds.) (1989). *Flunking grades: Research and policies on retention.* Philadelphia, PA: Falmer Press.

Stum, D.L. (1998). Five ingredients for an employee retention formula. *HR Focus,* 75(9), S9–S12.

Wendel, F.C., & Uerling, D.F. (1989). Assessment centers: Contributing to the preparation programs for principals. *NASSP Bulletin,* 73, 74–79.

Young, I.P. (2008). *The human resource function in educational administration.* 9th ed. Upper Saddle River, NJ: Pearson, Merrill Prentice Hall.

Student Personnel Services
It's Your Leadership That Counts

> **Primary chapter goal:**
>
> To underscore the significance of the assistant principal's role in supporting students, parents and school personnel in ensuring that each student has the opportunity to reach his or her potential.

The progress in schools across the country to provide student services to ensure that students succeed in school has been nothing but miraculous. Forty years ago many school systems in America did not have a program of special education for students with special learning needs. In fact, thousands of students with special needs were not in public school programs at all. It is common in schools today to have special services for all students. The Department of Student Services of the Washington County Public Schools (2014, May 11) clearly states, "The purpose of the Student Services Department is to support students, parents, and school personnel in ensuring that each student has the opportunity to mature to his or her full potential" (p. 1). Such services can be classified under two primary categories, direct services and special services.

Direct student services include those programs and activities available to all students such as guidance counseling, wellness services, educational planning, academic assistance, behavior intervention and support, social services, welfare services, homeless care services and others. **Special services** are those programs and activities provided for students with special needs such as physical disabilities, bipolar disorder, mental retardation, speech and language impairment, dyslexia, and others. These essential student services are discussed in this chapter.

Why Student Services in Schools? Isn't Learning the School's Job?

Title IX. Section 9101, (36) Pupil Services Personnel; Pupil Services—(A) Pupil Services Personnel—sets forth the following definition. "The term 'pupil services personnel' means school counselors, school social workers, school psychologists, and other qualified professional personnel involved in providing assessment, diagnosis, counseling, educational, therapeutic, and other necessary services as part of a comprehensive program to meet student needs." What student services are available in schools depends on several factors, from student needs to available funding.

Most schools commonly include some of the following student services:

Guidance and counseling

Speech and hearing

School health and welfare

Transportation assistance

Enrollment, attendance, truancy

Tutoring

Behavior, suspension

Home schooling

Student records

Intervention provisions

School safety and security

Dropout prevention

Social services

Career planning

Homeless liaison services

Academic advice

Work/study program

Testing/appraisal

Free lunch programs

Job placement

Parent counseling/training

Administrative assistance

Psychological services

Social work services

Mobility services

Special education

Occupational therapy

Gifted student program

Later in the chapter we will discuss services provided in special education programs. You most likely are keenly aware of such programs for physically disabled students, speech and hearing disabilities, mental retardation, learning disabilities and others, but contemporary schools have extended services for special needs students in several areas. Consider the matching quiz that follows. For each disability entry on the left, match it with its definition on the right.

You might not have majored in special education although your experience could have acquainted you with several of the terms in the quiz. If not,

Student Disability	Disability Definitions (not in correct order)
1. Attention Deficit Disorder	a. often characterized by difficulties with accurate word recognition, decoding. and spelling.
2. Asperger's Syndrome	b. makes careless mistakes, is easily distracted, fails to follow through on tasks.
3. Bipolar Disorder	c. causes involuntary sounds movements, vocal tics, blinking, jaw movements, jerking.
4. Tourette's Syndrome	d. severe multiple disabilities including speech, mobility, mental retardation, visual, physical, hearing and brain injury and others.
5. Dyslexia	e. bump, jolt, blow to head that disrupts normal brain function, goes from mild to serious amnesia.
6. Multi-handicapped Student	f. has difficulties with social, mental, physical and abnormal behavior. Considered as type of autism.
7. Learning/Disabled Gifted Student	g. depressed most of the day feeling sad, worthless, fatigued. Mood swings from low depression to high mania.
8. Neurological Impairments	h. highly gifted in one or more subject areas but deficient in others such as reading and writing.
9. Traumatic Brain Injury	i. disease of the nervous system that causes disruptions on one's level of functioning: cerebral palsy, multiple sclerosis, Alzheimer's disease.
10. Orthopedic Impairments	j. severe impairment that adversely affects a child's educational performance (e.g., polio, cerebral palsy, amputation).

as assistant principal, you will most likely experience students in the disability areas as defined in the quiz. The point in our follow-up program description of student services centers on the need for you, as assistant principal, to become knowledgeable of the nature of such services and your leadership role in supporting them.

Here are the answers to the matching quiz: 1–b, 2–f, 3–g, 4–c, 5–a, 6–d, 7–h, 8–i, 9–e, 10–j. We will discuss the topic of special student needs later in the chapter. The assistant principal's role in the area of student personnel services is of high import. One assistant school superintendent noted that, "the assistant school principal that can effectively supervise the pupil personnel function in the school will be a success."

What Competencies and Indicators Loom Important for Pupil Personnel Services?

Box 5.1 sets forth the major competencies and indicators of competencies for the assistant principal's task: To function as the school leader for pupil personnel services.

Box 5.1 Assistant Principal Competencies and Indicators: Student Personnel Services

Competency 1.0: Ability to manage and supervise the attendance procedures for the school

Indicators

1.1 Takes charge of the entire attendance operation from implementing board policy to computation of average daily membership (a.d.m.).

1.2 Works with computerized services for attendance reporting.

1.3 Supervises the procedure for follow-up on student absences.

1.4 Maintains a system for informing parents of student absences.

1.5 Establishes procedures for handling excessive student tardiness and absences.

1.6 Informs teachers of the legitimacy of student absences.

Competency 2.0: Ability to assess responsibility for all student management procedures.

Indicators

2.1 Takes leadership actions that serve to assess, evaluate and improve the climate of the school.

2.2 Works with the school principal, teachers, parents and students in establishing student behavior procedures in accordance with the school board policies and administrative regulations of the school district.

2.3 Works with teachers and students in the development of a student handbook that sets forth provisions for student services and expected student behavior.

2.4 Selects appropriate student disciplinary alternatives in accord with administrative regulations and school rules.

2.5 Works with the school principal in regard to establishing due process procedures for students who have committed behavioral violations and acts as the school representative at student disciplinary hearings.

Competency 3.0 Ability to supervise the school's guidance program.

Indicators

3.1 Develops guidelines for guidance personnel in relation to program scheduling, career development, self-assessment, testing, mentoring and other information relative to the student's strengths and interests.

3.2 Works with the guidance counselors in the development of a position description that centers on student performance and learning achievement.

3.3 Works cooperatively with the guidance staff in designing and implementing a school-testing program that meets federal, state and school board requirements.

Student Attendance and Student Achievement Results

After examining 156 study reports and abstracts of studies on the relationship between school attendance and student achievement, we can conclude that absence from school does negatively affect student academic performance. After all, there certainly is an assumed relationship between the two events; frequent absences from school logically would seem to reduce learning and lower scores on achievement tests. Yet, one gets the impression in examining the many study reports on the topic that the term "significant difference" is used rather loosely. It is not always clear what size sample was used in many studies and if only random, representative samples were used in the testing. A significant difference is a result that is not likely to occur randomly; rather the result shows that the relationship is actually causal; when one event occurs the other event occurs consistently as well. The change is not due to chance, but due directly to the relationship of the two events. The statistical relationship can be strong or weak. If the result "p" is less than 0.05, for example, the relationship probably is true.

What About Teacher Attendance? What Difference Does It Make?

If the school year consisted of 186 days and a teacher was absent for 18 days of the year would student achievement be affected? Most authorities would answer, "definitely, yes." Konz (2014, June 3) cited a report of the National Council on Teacher Quality indicating that teachers in forty school districts in 2012–13 missed 18 days or more of an average 186-day school year. "In schools where students are poorest and failing the most academically, teachers tend to be absent more often. In one study, the percentage of students reading below grade level was found to be the greatest predictor of school employee absenteeism" (Norton, 1998, p. 96).

Attempts to study solutions to reduce the incidence of teacher absenteeism are problematic for several reasons. Researchers find it difficult to control the many variables that accompany teacher absences. Attempting to relate teacher absences to student achievement is problematic as well. Considerations relevant to improving teacher absences have been suggested by authorities. Assistant school principals and principals might find the following recommendations beneficial:

1. School districts and local schools should develop specific guidelines for controlling employee absenteeism including policies and regulations that provide measures for dealing with excessive absence.

2. The local school should establish specific procedures for monitoring employee absences. Experience suggests that absenteeism is reduced when the employee is required to report their absence directly to their supervisor.

3. A system of personal counseling should be in place in cases of excessive absenteeism. In most cases, the cause of the absences can be identified and possibly obviated with the administration's support.

4. Schools should keep an ongoing record of absences and their "causes." In many cases, a positive intervention might be implemented that serves to reduce absences. For example, childcare provisions, parental care needs, or health care needs that are causing absences could be supported by the school.

5. Some school districts have found that a buy-back of unused sick leave tends to reduce teacher absences by discouraging indiscriminate use by employees. The monetary costs of such a program can be troublesome but could serve to keep quality teachers on the job.

Policy, Regulation and Rule: What's the Difference?

In dealing with school matters, the terms policy, regulation, rule and law frequently come into the conversation. It is not unusual for school leaders to use the terms policy, regulation and rule incorrectly. When establishing a procedure for students to follow in the school, for example, it is common that the comment, "that's our school policy on that matter," is used. We think it is important that school leaders know and use these terms in the proper way. **School district policy** adoption is the work of the school board. Only the school board can adopt school policy. All school systems have primary goals. Goals are statements of the major purposes for which the school exists. School policies are adaptations of the school system's goals. In this way, policies answer the question, "What to do?" That is, the school board is saying, this is what we want the school system to accomplish. One important characteristic of a school policy is that it is a general statement and leaves room for administrative discretion.

It has become more common for school board policies to be written verbatim from state law. This is because such matters as teacher dismissal, student suspension, hiring practices and other matters are often contested in court and failure of the school district to follow the law specifically is a common reason for the school to lose a legal case.

Administrative regulations, on the other hand, are specific statements that serve to answer the question, "How to do?" Although it is wise to have the school board give approval to administrative regulations, the school superintendent and professional staff are responsible for developing the regulations for carrying out the board's policies. Administrative regulations commonly are developed with input from the school community.

As assistant principal and school leader you should know the differences among the foregoing terms and use them correctly in your work. It is not uncommon for one to hear a school assistant principal or principal to speak of their school policies when they actually are referring to the school rules.

The local school develops **school rules** that deal with matters of student conduct, student absences, grading procedures, student activities, safety matters and so forth. Nevertheless, school rules tie closely to administrative regulations as fits the case. It is clear that school rules cannot be contrary to the school district's administrative regulations. In the same way, administrative regulations cannot be contrary to school board policies nor can school board policies be contrary to state and national laws.

A limited example of each of the foregoing terms is as follows:

a. *School board policy (limited excerpt):* The school superintendent and persons delegated by superintendent are given the responsibility for determining the personnel needs of the school district and recruiting qualified candidates to recommend for employment to the board. Efforts should be implemented to recruit a varied group of personnel relative to experience, competency and background preparation. All qualified candidates shall be considered regardless of race, national origin, age, sex, creed or marital status. The school superintendent and/or other delegated administrator in the school district must assume the responsibility for ensuring that each candidate meets the qualifications for the position of nomination according to state laws and school board policies.

b. *School district administrative regulation (limited excerpt):* Written applications, official transcriptions of college work, student teaching and teaching reports and recommendations, and personnel interviews provide the primary data for personnel selection. The posting of position openings will be appropriately distributed by the central personnel office of the school district and through the offices of the school principals in the district as fits the case. The central human resources office will screen the list of applicants and send its recommendations to the school principal for employment consideration. Qualified applicants will be interviewed by telephone or in person and finalists will be identified and interviewed in person by the school principal and/or assistant principal. Recommendations for employment will be sent to the central human resources office and to the school superintendent for final approval before being recommended to the school board for final hiring approval.

c. *Local school rule (limited excerpt):* All teachers new to the school will be given an experienced mentor to provide guidance relative to matters of orientation such as availability of instructional resources, student grading, required reports, in-service program activities and other matters that meet the teacher's needs. The mentoring services for new teachers will be continued for as long as the teacher and school administration view it as necessary. The mentoring process is considered as a planned and organized process whereby positive ongoing support activities are cooperatively determined.

Descriptions of Various Student Services That Assistant Principals Will Encounter as Related to Student Guidance and Counseling Services

Student guidance and counseling services have witnessed major changes during the last two decades. This transformation has gone from limited services in student scheduling and testing activities to programs of continuous improvements that are embedded in the school's curriculum. Guidance and counseling has become a comprehensive development program that is integral to the development of all students in order for them to reach their optimal development. Additionally, guidance and counseling services are no longer a program primarily relegated to the high school level for student scheduling and career planning, rather it is a developmental program that supports the student's personal, social, academic, and career development through all grades K–12.

Who carries out the guidance and counseling program? Not only guidance counselors who lead a comprehensive development program that includes the diverse needs of many students as well as the personal, social, psychological and academic needs of all students. Along with school counselors, teachers, principals and assistant principals, school district administrators, and the school board play integral roles in the planning and implementation of a quality counseling and guidance program; all members and agencies contribute to the program's mission.

Guidance and counseling is not just a number of student services performed in the school, rather it is an integral part of the student's educational program throughout his or her school experiences. It is common to read and hear that today's comprehensive guidance and counseling programs provide opportunities for each and every student to learn to live, to learn to learn and to learn to work. It addresses the social, intellectual, emotional and psychological needs of each student with the goal of increasing the student's knowledge of self, identifying his or her own strengths and interests, and providing opportunities for them to reach their optimal development.

Personal success in life is dependent in large part on knowing one's self. The individual's values and beliefs set the foundation for his or her personal standards in pursuing goals and objectives. Thus, understanding self, appreciating others, coping with life's challenges, decision making, facing change and becoming a productive citizen loom important in a successful life. Taking charge of one's own education and developing guidelines that center on life-long learning are personal needs for every student. Along with the academic knowledge required for success, attention to decision-making skills, problem solving, reasoning and critical thinking underscore the theme of learning to learn. Each of the foregoing skills ties directly to life's requirements of the world of work and a meaningful life. With continuous learning and educational advancements, more doors open and personal independence advances. Students who learn to work tend to grow and develop as productive citizens. Historically, we have lived to work. Now, we desire a more balanced work life and our goals are centered on working to live.

The school assistant principal cooperates with school counselors in the designing and delivering of a quality guidance program and then continues to assist counselors in implementing the program plan. The foundations for a successful program rest on the belief that all children are unique personalities and that every child can be successful in relation to lifelong learning, gaining a positive self-image, and being an active and productive citizen in the home and school community.

What Personnel Services Can Be Accomplished at the Elementary School Level? Middle School Level? Secondary School Level?

Elementary school children must be provided services from a personal, social, and academic level. Learning how to cope with the new and somewhat complex kindergarten requirements indeed can be troublesome for some children. Social, personal and academic skills all come into play in learning how to live with others in this new environment of school.

How to deal with all the other kids and learning how to decide what I am supposed to do when I have to use the restroom is important for children in these early years. Learning the difference between work and play and not always having someone to do a task for me, like at home, calls for decision making that I really did not have to do so much at home. A fire drill and I am supposed to lead the class to safety in the playground area. Decisions, decisions—I need some guidance!

At the middle school level, the developing adolescent needs of students must be addressed. Social competence becomes increasingly important. Personal interests and strengths become important in thinking about course pursuits and ultimate school graduation. What special skills need to be considered and how these strengths tie to ultimate career plans are becoming more important. At the high school level, understanding self, one's strengths and interests, and obvious talents call for a realistic plan for graduation and potential career pursuits. A realistic plan to succeed is in order. Decision-making responsibilities become more apparent and assuming personal responsibility for one's education is evident. Guidance and counseling are needed to accomplish the desired ends. A balanced program of experiences and activities must be determined and a systematic learning program must be planned and implemented on the part of each student.

Components for a successful guidance and counseling program include a guided curriculum, individual planning and professional development activities. A guided curriculum consists of structured experiences through the grades in relation to decision-making skills, knowledge of self and meaningful career development. The student's personal academic achievements, strengths and interests serve as the focus for individual career planning. Responsive services center on immediate student needs and concerns. Parental involvement at this time is essential. The assistant principal provides administrative support throughout the entire planning process, and works cooperatively with planning program teams, community services and other research teams to ensure that best practices are being implemented.

Although planning takes much time and effort on the part of all concerned in the process, the student benefits are witnessed in improved academic performance, a realistic career development plan, improved problem-solving skills, a better understanding of self, improved personal relationships, and a better understanding of our changing world. Parents benefit by creating new partnerships with school personnel, community service agencies and an improved knowledge of the important work of the school's guidance and counseling program.

The school administration benefits by the creation of a relevant program of guidance and counseling. Program evaluation and program accountability are more valid and reliable, student needs are met and the proactive work of the school administration has resulted in an improved school climate. Teachers, school boards and the local business community each benefit by an effective guidance and counseling program. For example, local businesses have an improved work force potentially available that understands the needed standards of business; new links with the school and school district are established; a better understanding of the school's mission is realized and improved communication with the school results.

Box 5.2 includes several competencies and related indicators of competencies that apply to the school's guidance and counseling program. Each competency holds implications for the work of the guidance counselors and the assistant school principal. The competencies and indicators serve a good purpose for examining the school's guidance and counseling program and checking its accountability factors for reporting and improvement purposes.

Box 5.2 Competencies and Indicators of Competencies for the School's Guidance and Counseling Program

Competency 1.0 Ability to plan and implement a structured and developmental guidance and counseling program in an organized way for individual and group activities in grades K-12.

Indicators of Competency

1.1 The specific individual student academic, social, psychological and career needs are identified and duly considered in the planning and implementation of guidance and counseling programs for individual students and student groups.

1.2 The curriculum standards for student achievement and personal conduct are addressed in the planning of each guidance and counseling program and activity.

1.3 The guidance and counseling program activities are planned in terms of the specific interests and needs of students as determined by a variety of assessment strategies.

1.4 A record of time spent on the guidance and counseling program activities is accurately maintained by the assistant school principal.

Competency 2.0 Ability to provide easy access to guidance and counseling services for students that are most helpful to them in dealing with their personal needs related to the academic, social and career issues facing them.

Indicators of Competency

2.1 Guidance and counseling curriculum materials show that both individual and group services are available in the school's program and that referral services are in place and utilized.

2.2 The local school board has adopted specific guiding policies for the implementation of the school district's guidance and counseling program and the local school(s) is following the administrative procedures for the guidance and counseling program in its practices.

2.3 The opportunities for ongoing in-service development in the area of guidance and counseling are available for all counselors and teachers including data information regarding student progress, pupil development and program results.

2.4 Accountability measures in relation to time spent by school personnel on guidance and counseling activities are retained by the school assistant principal and used for adjusting schedules and assignments in the area of guidance and counseling.

Competency 3.0 Ability to provide ample opportunities for teachers, parents, students and others to participate in the development and monitoring of career plans for students.

Indicators of Competency

3.1 There is an identifiable K-12 guidance and counseling program in progress in the school district and appropriately administered in each individual school in the district.

3.2 The career development program as required in your state is identifiably in place and successful.

3.3 Necessary career information is relevant and readily available to students.

3.4 The leadership of the assistant principal and guidance counselors is revealed in part by the time being spent on career planning for students.

Competency 4.0 Ability to plan and implement a comprehensive guidance and counseling program in the school that is led by qualified school administrators and purposeful goals and objectives.

Indicators of Competency

4.1 The leadership of the school and guidance counselors is active in school district programs and committees that center on student services.

4.2 An identifiable and relevant program of in-service guidance and counseling activities is available to all members of the school faculty.

4.3 A meaningful program of information relating to the purposes of the guidance and counseling program in the school is ongoing.

4.4 Specifically planned need assessments relative to the program of guidance and counseling are identified and the required competencies are pursued.

4.5 Time spent on program activities is on record and evaluated in terms of returns on investment.

4.6 A comprehensive guidance and counseling program has been officially adopted by the school district's board of education.

4.7 All school counselors are certificated and highly qualified for the program of guidance and counseling.

4.8 Approved job descriptions for school counselors are in place and the role of the school assistant principal in the guidance and counseling program is specifically addressed in the role's position description.

4.9 The school district's and school's budgets provide the resources and facilities needed to carry out the guidance and counseling educational program.

Competency 6.0 Ability to implement the guidance and counseling program as an integral part of the school's total educational program.

Indicators of Competency

6.1 Evidence is available to verify that collaboration among guidance counselors, teachers, assistant principal and principal, is in place.

6.2 Data are available that verify that program assessments have been used to identify program priorities in the area of guidance and counseling.

6.3 The school's mission goals and objectives make it clear that program standards established by government agencies and the board of education are included in the school's comprehensive guidance and counseling program.

Responsive Services of Importance to the Student Services Program

Effective student programs depend on a variety of responsive services. In providing effective leadership to your school's student services program, you will be involved in ongoing consultation with parents, teachers, guidance counselors and other educators in the school district and members of the school community. This task represents your primary responsibility as assistant principal, to coordinate the counseling and intervention services being recommended for individual students. Is each of the several entities "in tune" regarding the guidance and counseling plan for the student at hand? Is the student's plan being carried out effectively by each instructional component that is participating? What progress is in evidence?

What time is being spent on personal counseling with students, including small and large group instructional counseling? Are the counseling services being provided for all students and not just problem cases? Crisis counseling becomes important in emergency cases when such interventions as referral services are needed. Referrals are common in cases of mental health needs, employment placements in work-study programs, vocational rehabilitation, juvenile and social services. How are such responsive services being carried out, followed up and resolved?

Responsive system support for students also necessitates your best leadership and collaboration with other individuals and agencies. Such support services include a wide variety of student problems related to student dropout prevention, student–teacher relationships, bullying, grief, substance abuse, family disputes and the inability of the student to cope with problems faced as a young child or youth. Let's take time to look at the school dropout problem and the leadership that is needed to reduce and/or prevent it.

A Lightbulb Experience—Student Dropouts: Nothing Can Really Be Done About It, Or Can It?

"Every 29 seconds, another student gives up on school, resulting in more than one million American dropouts a year—or 7,000 every day" (National Center for Educational Statistics, May 23, 2014, p. 3). Furthermore, the National Center points out that students from low-income families are 2.4 times more likely to drop out of school than are children from middle-income families and 10.5 times more likely than students from high-income families. In addition, students with disabilities are also more likely to drop out; it is estimated that 36.4 percent of disabled youth drop out of school before completing a diploma or certificate. Although statistics do differ, research evidence indicates that student retention rates are approximately 66.1 percent to 74.4 percent (Barton, 2005).

Legters (May 23, 2014) points out several key factors that are associated with student dropouts. Poor grades in core subjects, low attendance, retention in grade, disengagement from learning and behavioral problems lead the list. The National Center for Educational Statistics (May 23, 2014) adds three more causal factors: the student moves location during high school, the student comes from a single parent family, and the student feels that no adult in the school cares about his or her welfare. Now, let's ask which of the several key factors associated with student dropouts can you, as assistant principal, do nothing about? Perhaps you could be excused from the reason that the student changes locations during his or her school years or that the student comes from a single parent family.

Nevertheless, the other factors provide ample opportunities for you to implement your best leadership qualities in reducing the dropout rate in your school. A major problem facing school leaders in regard to reducing school dropout rates centers on the seemingly contradictory factors of

> facing the demands of federal, state and local educational agencies for higher and more rigorous standards of student achievement, while at the same time being asked to reduce the student dropout rate. Nevertheless, proactive leadership can serve positive purposes in ameliorating some of the reasons that underlie student dropouts from school.

A Look at Interventions and Possible Retention Solutions

If the solution to the student dropout problem were simple, perhaps the problem would have been resolved long ago. As the Association for Supervision and Curriculum Development (May 24, 2014) points out, "The extra efforts that schools make to support students in all these circumstances will likely determine whether schools achieve higher or lower high school completion rates than expected" (p. 3).

There is a realistic need for schools to find a way to gain the services of more personnel to serve individual students. Voluntary services of retired teachers, college and university personnel and other "qualified" community members to guide, counsel and mentor individual students should be assessed in your school community. Retired persons from various occupational fields could be utilized to interact with individual students and provide motivation for the student's retention in school. More school counselors must be supported through federal and state educational funding programs, including research grants. Some community businesses, industries or clubs might be instrumental in providing funds for a student retention program or providing a "scholarship" for hiring an additional school counselor.

Such efforts serve to reduce the common high student/teacher ratios in schools and provide more one-on-one counseling sessions for the guidance counselor and student. Empirical evidence suggests that guidance and counseling personnel are spending the lion's share of available time on matters relating to student class scheduling, counseling students on university pursuits, test administration and evaluation, and other supervisory tasks such as lunchroom duty and hall duty.

Some school districts have become involved in programs such as "Communities in Schools," whose primary purpose is that of student retention in school. Partnerships within the school community collaborate in order to provide some services and resources for the program. Volunteer mentoring services, tutoring services, occupational guidance, work-study programs, special student awards, work-life skill instruction, after-school programs and a variety of other student services exemplify such programs. Not all such activities center specifically on academic or social instruction. Rather, student interest sessions that center on dance classes, hot-rods, art and music, computers, bicycle repair, modeling and others are designed to meet student interest and foster their continuation in school programs.

One program in Phoenix, Arizona focuses on bicycle repair skills. Bicycles needing repair are donated to the program and students volunteer to learn how to repair them and place them back on the road. After so much time as a repair volunteer, the student receives a bike free of charge. According to the program director, Clair Sutter, the students not only gain new mechanical knowledge and skills, but the student's educational interests are facilitated as well.

Legters (May 23, 2014) points out several useful student retention strategies: a school within a school for greater personalization, partnerships between high schools, feeder middle schools, ninth grade transitions programs, and special support for special needs students outside of school time.

A Step-by-Step Plan for Reducing Student Dropouts

Tasks and responsibilities for school assistant principals commonly differ from school level to school level and from school district to school district. The assistant school principal should not be expected to perform all of the tasks and have all of the administrative competencies set forth in this text. The competencies and standards set forth for the assistant principal should be viewed as those that represent standards for performance and those that the assistant school principal might perform, other administrators might perform, or those that the assistant principal might supervise. In some cases, the service might be led by the school principal or by teacher leaders in the school. In other instances, the services might be outsourced or performed by a special team of school-district members.

In any case, the following provisions will serve as guidelines for planning, initiating, implementing and evaluating an action program to increase student graduation results. The literature is filled with programs and ideas regarding how to resolve the student dropout problem. However, as noted by Shannon and Bylsma (2005), there has been no significant program discovered that assures the prevention of student dropouts. Nevertheless, many concepts and practices presented in the several chapters of this book recommend many of the prevention strategies presented by researchers and other authorities. For example, the topic of school climate has been featured throughout the book. Five general considerations for you to consider in your efforts to improve student retention in your school are as follows:

1. Create a school environment that is attractive, caring, warm and supportive.
2. Be certain that students are able to obtain social, health, academic and other supportive resources that help them obviate barriers to their learning and meet their personal interests and emergent needs.

3. Individualize learning programs that are challenging but connect with the student's special interests and successful learning level.

4. Make special efforts to provide opportunities for students to learn by doing and ways in which their learning connects with their present and future interests.

5. Give students the opportunity to relate personally with a variety of caring adults both within and outside the school environment.

6. Encourage each member of your school staff to become a student advocate, one who is student centered and considers the special needs of all students.

Leadership Requirements for Serving Students with Special Needs

Our final chapter consideration centers on the assistant school principal's need to understand the comprehensive program activities of the school's program for students with special needs. We begin with a quiz that gives you a chance to "test" your general knowledge about special education in school settings.

Quiz on Special Education in the Local School

Directions: Answer true or false to each of the following statements. Do not guess the answer. Rather, just skip the ones that you are not certain about.

1. Empirical evidence and basic research results suggest that school assistant principals and principals most often are not prepared to oversee the special education program in their school. ___T ___F

2. Even though special education has been implemented in schools nationally, neither the United States government offices nor state legislatures have provided guidance/requirements for implementing special education administration for the local schools in America. ___T ___F

3. In spite of the fact that services for students with disabilities have been implemented in schools for more than thirty years, present services basically have been limited to the physically disabled, speech and language impairments, deaf and hearing impairments and learning disabled students. ___T ___F

4. School principals, by law, are required to find disabled children in their school district and report their findings to the proper authorities. ___T ___F

5. The IEP for students with special needs refers to "Internal and External Placement" of students with special needs in various learning environments. ___T ___F

6. IDEA, as related to special needs program in local schools, stressed the purposes of supporting special needs students or "Identify, Diagnose, Examine, and Assess." ___T ___F

7. Since the special needs of many students in local schools necessitate special attention, authorities recommend that the school assistant principal and principal leave the administration of special needs programs to other, more prepared, specialists. ___T ___F

8. Although the topic of tasks and related administrative competencies for special education for the assistant school principal and principal have been considered by various national associations, a viable list of specific tasks and competencies for these administrative roles for the special education program have yet to be developed. ___T ___F

9. National research studies on the school assistant principal and principal have found that less than 5 percent of their time is being spent on the administration of the special education program. ___T ___F

10. One special student needs program in schools centers on students with dyslexia. Dyslexia is a language processing disorder that results in a difficulty to read fluently and inhibits the ability to comprehend. ___T ___F

How do you think you scored on the quiz? If you answered 9–10 correctly, you did especially well and are qualified to skip the next section of the chapter. A score of 7–8 correct answers is very good as well, congratulations. Five to six correct answers is good, but you can benefit by examining the following section of the chapter. A score of 4 or less should not be discouraging for you. You'll find the next section of the chapter most beneficial.

Quiz answers: 1–T, 2–F, 3–F, 4–T, 5–F, 6–F, 7–F, 8–F, 9–F, 10–T.

An Examination of the Answers to the Special Education Quiz

Statement 1 is true. "Both research and empirical evidence support the contention that school principals are not adequately prepared to oversee the special-education program in their schools" (Norton et al., 2012, p. 94). That is, research suggests that most school administrators lack the course work and field experience needed to lead local efforts to create learning environments that emphasize a successful program for students with disabilities (DiPaola & Tschannen-Moran, 2003). Many new building administrators find themselves in new situations that call for decisions on matters related to unfamiliar issues such as IEPs, 504 rulings, due process hearings, and IDEA compliance requirements. Yet, empirical evidence suggests that the attitude and leadership of the school administrators are essential to an effective special education program. Administrative preparation programs commonly provide few or no specifics on the topic of special education, and educators tend to report that what they do know is learned while on the job.

Statement 2 is false. The federal government passed the Education for All Handicapped Children Act (EAHCA) in 1975. Section 504 of the Rehabilitation Act of 1973 established the requirement that all students, regardless of any disability, could not be discriminated against or excluded from participation in or denied the benefits of any program activity receiving federal funds. Participation in such programs as physical education, athletics, school plays, art and music was no exception; disabled students were to be included. Inclusion in the least restricted environment placed every student in the regular classroom with few exceptions.

Statement 3 is false. Comprehensive school programs of special education course work commonly include as many as twelve different special services. These services are carried out by a number of special programs (e.g., social work, home schooling, rehabilitation, occupational therapy, referral services, medical services and many others).

Statement 4 is true. The Individuals with Disabilities Act of 1990 stipulates that public school districts must identify students with disabilities within their jurisdiction whether or not the student is attending a public school.

Statement 5 is false. IEP stands for Individualized Educational Program and is a requirement for all students in the school's special needs program. It represents an instructional plan for the disabled student and is used as an "accountability instrument" for assessing and evaluating a student's learning progress. In brief, the IEP includes the individually structured educational plan for the student, content, instructional methods, and measures of achievement necessary for determining the least restricted placement of the student in the curricular program (Norton et al., 2012).

Statement 6 is false. IDEA (the Individualized Disabilities Education Act), enacted in 1990, was established to make certain that all special needs students had equal access and opportunity to participate in an appropriate, free public school program. The federal legislation set forth special requirements concerning the placement of special needs students in appropriate programs and activities. That is, program placements must be appropriate to the individual student's educational goals and assure continued progress in the curriculum of the school.

Statement 7 is false. On the contrary, both empirical and basic research strongly suggest that school administrators must take the lead in order that special education programs are successful. This leadership includes participation in the development of school district policies and administrative regulations that pertain to the planning, designing, administration and evaluation of special education program activities.

Statement 8 is false. A number of research authorities, federal, state and local education agencies has developed comprehensive statements of the tasks, competencies and indicators of competencies required of assistant school principals and principals in the area of special education. In 2003, Norton researched and reported the required tasks and competencies in special education for both administrative positions. For example, within the task of functioning as the school leader for pupil personnel services, the assistant school principal's required competencies included: the ability to establish ongoing special education program development opportunities. Selected indicators of competencies included: (1) released time is provided for the staff to attend special education conferences, meet with special education personnel, observe colleague's classrooms, and engage in independent research on special education; (2) professional development activities for faculty personnel are directly applicable to practice; (3) professional growth and development programs and activities in special education for faculty personnel are in concert with the school's mission statement, especially in regard to the objectives for special education and the needs of student with disabilities; (4) meetings are held with the special education staff, parents of children with disabilities, and others to stress the importance of the school's mission statement especially referencing its meaning for comprehensive programs for all students; and (5) encouragement is given to staff members to participate in special education development activities.

Statement 9 is false. Empirical evidence suggests that special education programs and activities consume 30 percent of the school administrator's total work time. Effective administrative support is considered as essential to successful special education program activities. Gersten et al. (2001) concluded "that local administrative support and other general educators had major effects on all critical aspects of special-education teachers' working conditions" (p. 557). All authorities tend to agree that effective school principals invest the necessary time to develop administrative procedures that enhance the ability of teachers to perform their instructional tasks toward the goal of improved student academic performance.

Statement 10 is true. Dyslexia is one of the several student disabilities that the assistant principal will encounter in his or her administrative role. Other student disabilities that are commonly encountered by local schools include bipolar disorder, Tourette's syndrome, Asperger's syndrome, traumatic brain injury, disabled/gifted student, ADD, and others.

Personnel problems in the area of special education include the ongoing loss of qualified school counselors. The shortage of qualified special education teachers has been a continuing problem. Statistics reveal that approximately one half of special education teachers leave the field within the first three years. Reportedly, the lack of retention is due to poor administrative support, poor preparation, complexity of the position responsibilities, and the overwhelming paperwork requirements (Billingsley & Cross, 1991). Although some states have approved provisional teaching certificates for special education teachers, many leave the position three years before the certification deadline. The earlier position responsibilities of student counseling and work-study programs no longer meet the program needs of a comprehensive guidance and counseling program.

Snapshot 5.1—If You Want to Know What Students Are Thinking, Just Ask Them!

Our study team was asked to visit a local school district and try to assess the climate in the schools, grades K–12. The district school board had concerns about reports of unsatisfactory student behavior and wanted the study team to get "at the roots" of the problems and make recommendations for the needed improvement. There had been a "food fight" in the cafeteria of one high school; students in one middle school had a sit-in protest against their school's newly adopted homework regulations; and the sixth-grade students of an elementary school were having problems related to bullying and extortion of lunch money.

On one occasion, three members of the elementary school assessment team met with a class of sixth-grade students to discuss purposes of the visit and gain whatever input that might be received from the elementary school student group. After a brief introduction regarding the problems being faced at the elementary school, one team member asked, "What do you pupils see as the major reason for the problems that we have heard about at your school?" Almost in chorus, the hands of virtually every student shot up in the air with the resounding response, "Dickie Jackson!" We contend that students are quite capable of stating their views and giving information regarding their personal strengths, needs and interests. If you want to know what students think, ask them!

Box 5.3 is an example of a student assessment survey form that could be adjusted for the various grade levels as necessary and implemented in your school.

Box 5.3 Student Personnel Survey Form

Directions: Provide your answer of "yes" or "no" for each of the questions listed below. Before answering each question, give a moment's thought to your personal experience regarding the item and write in a brief response to clarify your feelings on the matter.

1. Have you used the school's guidance and counseling services this year?
   ___Yes ___No

2. If you have had any contacts with the guidance and counseling services this year (including class scheduling, testing services, job or career counseling, academic program counseling), were these services helpful for you? ___Yes ___No

3. Do you feel that you are well acquainted with the student services available to you through our guidance and counseling services department? ___Yes ___No

4. Is there anything that you would like to discuss in a private talk with a school counselor? ___Yes ___No

5. Are there any special curriculum areas or other school matters that you would like to talk about? ___Yes ___No

6. At this point in time, do you look forward to coming to school each day? ___Yes ___No

7. Are you genuinely concerned about how other students feel about you? ___Yes ___No

8. Would you like to know much more about the occupational areas that you are most interested in at this time? ___Yes ___No

9. Have you personally encountered problems of bullying, peer pressure, student relationships, or other such problems this year in school? ___Yes ___No

10. Do you believe that the school year thus far has been positive relative to your own academic achievement? ___Yes ___No

11. Take a minute or two to tell us about any other ideas and/or matters that you wish in regard to the school's guidance and counseling program and/or other matters such as ways that the program might better serve you.

_____

_____

_____

_____

_____

Your Name: _____ (optional)

Grade Level _____

Summary

Student personnel services focus on a comprehensive program of activities that serve to support the school's mission of helping each student reach his or her potential. An effective student services program serves all students in providing opportunities to become involved in direct guidance and counseling experiences that lead to a better understanding of self and also give special attention to meeting the needs of students with special needs. The student personnel services program is important at all levels of the school's program, K–12. Learning to live, learning to learn, and learning to work hold implications for instruction at the outset of the student's education.

The direct and special programs provided by the school require qualified personnel to administer student services, as well as effective administrative leadership to support guidance counselors and others in the attainment of their responsibilities. Early programs of guidance and counseling commonly emphasized activities centering on class scheduling and career considerations. Contemporary student services programs extend far beyond these important activities and deal with an ever-expanding list of student development programs and activities, along with programs centering on students with special needs.

Effective student services programs are guided by federal, state, school district and local school board laws, policies, administrative regulations and school rules. Research and empirical evidence has developed relevant tasks, competencies and indicators of competencies for directing the necessary leadership of the assistant school principal and others in administering student personnel services. The need for assistant principals to become highly qualified for administering the student services program is evident. Continuous involvement in professional growth and development in student services activities for assistant school principals is now a position requirement.

The program of student personnel services must be tied to the overall mission of the school and have the purpose of fostering an improved learning climate for all students. An effective program is curriculum embedded, meaning that it serves the goals and objectives of the school's mission. In this sense, all school personnel, teachers and administrators, hold guidance and counseling responsibilities.

The student personnel services program must give special attention to school problems that center on the serious matter of student dropouts. Leadership action is required to establish a planned program to deal with dropout reduction. Chapter 5 has set forth several recommendations in this respect. However, what is needed is leadership action that establishes a plan to remediate student dropouts, action to implement the plan with personnel resources that serve to carry out the plan, and specific strategies for assessing and evaluating the plan's effectiveness.

Before moving on to Chapter 6, give thought to the implications of Chapter 5 for improvements in your school or the school in which you will become assistant principal. What priorities relative to student personnel services would be set forth? How would you lead in involving your entire staff toward the realization of the paramount importance of their role in fostering an effective student personnel program? What do you need to do to ensure a personal, ongoing program of professional development in the area of student services?

Discussion Questions

1. What is the status of your school's student personnel services program or one with which you are most familiar? To what extent are the services comprehensive and tied to the primary objectives of your school's misson? Is the school district's student personnel services program a K–12 curriculum embedded program? What leadership actions might an assistant school principal assume to improve the student services program as needed?

2. Give consideration to the effectiveness of your school's student personnel services program. What specific steps, if any, have been implemented to assess the program's accountability? If needed, what steps would you recommend?

3. Examine the program provisions of your school's student personnel services or a school with which you are most familiar. Use a checklist of the various services discussed in Chapter 5 to give you some idea regarding the comprehensiveness of your school's program.

4. Review the chapter's discussion on gaining input from students or parents or others regarding the services provided in your school's student services program. Develop a survey questionnaire similar to the one presented in Chapter 5 and administer it to the appropriate group. See if you are not surprised with the responses received.

CASE STUDIES

Case 5.1 I Wonder What Ever Happened to Noah

Noah Hernandez was a junior student at Viewpoint High School. His academic grades were above average in every subject and he possessed outstanding skills in the area of air science. Noah lived with his mother and two brothers on a small farm just outside the city limits of Viewpoint, Lafayette. He did participate in the after school football program. His later after school hours were spent on the farm doing various farm chores; early morning time was spent feeding and milking cows and performing gardening chores on one acre of farm land. Noah lost his father one year ago.

It was early in the following year when Noah was to be in grade 11. However, Noah had not shown up for school that year. During a meeting of the school principal, assistant principal, athletics director and guidance counselor, questions of student tardiness, absenteeism and student dropouts came to the floor.

"Our student absenteeism has increased by quite a lot compared to the same time last year," inserted Assistant Principal Melanie Millen. "And I have handled more tardies this semester than ever before," she said.

"Three of my football team members did not return to school this year," reported Coach Emory. "Roberto Cortez moved with his family to Nebraska and another, Andy Morton, reportedly gained permission to join the military service. But I don't know whatever happened to Noah Hernandez."

"Yes, what did happen to Noah?" responded Counselor Tom Sweeney. "He was one of our good students."

"Well, I think we need to find out about our school's student retention rates. Statistics indicate that retention rates nationally are somewhere in the 60 percents," said Principal Scott.

Discussion

Consider case 5.1 and provide your views of the matter at hand at Viewpoint High School. What appears to be the "real situation" at the school relative to tardies, attendance and student dropouts? What is the status of the administrative leadership and what actions should be given priority consideration?

Case 5.2 What Are the Alternatives, If Any?

Office of the School Superintendent
District of Mont View
MEMO
To: All Local School Administrators
From: Elaine Ora, Superintendent
RE: Reduction of Staff/Programs: Your immediate response is required

Due to the reduction in the school district's student enrollment and increasing expenditures for personnel compensation and related school expenses, the school board has directed me to reduce school expenditure "considerably" for the following school year.

Rather than have each school administration reduce expenditures randomly, I am ordering expenditures in each school to give priority to three program areas. The three areas are presented in priority order.

I regret having to reduce our programs in any way; each program is important to our mission's success. Nevertheless, the defeat of our recent finance issue by the voters in the community leaves us no choice but to do so.

Priority reduction program areas will be as follows:

1. Reduction of full-time kindergarten to one-half time.
2. Reduction of the student guidance and counseling program services, including the number of counselors at each school.
3. Reduction of attendance at all professional conferences and workshops.
4. Reduction of teacher aides at all school levels.

None of these reductions will be easy to do or to "sell" to the parents and members of our school community. Please know that I will assume the responsibility for communicating the matter to our local parent/teacher organization and other agencies that will be concerned.

Discussion

Note carefully what is being asked of you regarding case 5.2. You are asked to consider *only item number 2* of the superintendent's request, that of the reduction of the school's guidance and counseling program including the reduction of guidance counseling personnel. Assume that you are the assistant principal of an elementary school in the school district that has only one guidance counselor. Assume also that the guidance counselor position is to be terminated and that the laws of the state permit such actions due to budget cuts required by law. Your task is to design a plan to continue the primary responsibilities of the school's guidance and counseling services to the fullest extent possible using only the present resources available to the school. For example, how might a number of the required guidance and counseling services be delegated to other "qualified" personnel in your school?

References

ASCD (1990). Choose effective approaches to staff development. An excerpt from chapter 12 of *Elementary school science for the 90's* by Susan Loucks-Horsley and Roxanne Kapitan. Alexandria, VA: Association of Supervision and Curriculum Development.

Barton, P. (2005, January). Unfinished business: More measured approaches in standard-based reform (Policy Information Report). Princeton, NJ: Education Testing Service, Policy Information Center.

Billingsley, B.S., & Cross, L.H. (1991). Teachers' decisions to transfer from special to general education. *The Journal of Special Education*, 25, 453–471.

DiPaola, M.F., & Tschannen-Moran, M. (2003). The principal at a crossroad: A study of the conditions and concerns of principals. *NASSP Bulletin*, 87(634), 43–65.

EAHCA (1975). The Education for All Handicapped Children Act was an amendment to the Education Act for All Handicapped Children of 1974. The federal law is now Public Law 94–142. The law provided for appropriate education for those children not receiving proper education.

Gersten, R., Fuchs, L., Williams, J., & Baker, S. (2001). Teaching reading comprehension to students with learning disabilities: A review of research. *Review of Research*, 71, 279–320.

IDEA, Individuals with Disabilities Act (1990). Federal Government Act, Section 612, P.L. 105-17. Children with disabilities are entitled to a free appropriate education.

Konz, A. (2014, June 3). Teachers absent from class way too much, study says. *USA Today*. Report of a study by the National Council on Teacher Quality. From the web: www.usatoday.com/story/new/nation/2014/06/03/teachers-attendance-study/9889949

Legters, N. (2014, May 23). Dropout prevention. *Ask the Expert*. National High School Center for the American Institutes for Research, Washington, D.C. From the web: file:///Users.Scott. Desktop/High%20School%Dropout%20Problem%20and%20Prevention.webarchive

National Center for Educational Statistics (2014, May 23). *Background on high school dropouts*. From the web: file:///Scott/Desktop/Background%20on%High%20School%20Dropouts%20%7C%Do%20Something.webarchive

Norton, M.S. (2008). *Human resources administration for educational leaders*. Thousand Oaks, CA: Sage.

Norton, M.S. (2003). *Competency based preparation of educational administrators: Tasks, competencies, and indicators of competencies*. Division of Educational Leadership and Policy Studies, College of Education, Arizona State University. Tempe, AZ: Author (Ed.).

Norton, M.S. (1998). Teacher absenteeism: A growing dilemma in education. *Contemporary Education*, 69(2), 95.

Norton, M.S., Kelly, L.K., & Battle, A.R. (2012). *The principal as student advocate: A guide for doing what's best for all students*. Larchmont, NY: Eye On Education.

Rehabilitation Act of 1973. The national law protects qualified individuals from discrimination based on their disabilities. The Act was amended in 1992 to stipulate that the term "individuals with disabilities" does not include individuals who are currently in the illegal use of drugs.

Shannon, G.G., & Bylsma, P. (2005). *Promising programs and practices for dropout prevention*. Report to the Legislature, Office of the Superintendent of Public Schools, Olympia, WA.

Washington County Public Schools (2014). Student Services. *Building a community that inspires curiosity, creativity, and achievement*. Hagerstown, MD: Rick Akers, Director of Secondary Schools and Student Services. www.wcps.k12.md.us

A Resource File of Tasks, Competencies, and Indicators of Competencies for the Position of Assistant School Principal

Perfecting the Leadership Position

Primary chapter goal:

To provide a resource compendium of the primary tasks, competencies and indicators of competencies for the position of assistant school principal that serve as guidelines and standards for achieving excellence in the role.

The Purposes of the Chapter

As the primary chapter goal suggests, this chapter will focus on a comprehensive compendium of tasks, competencies and indicators of competencies for the assistant school principal. The selected tasks for the position represent an in-depth analysis of numerous contemporary position descriptions, surveys of the opinions of practicing assistant school principals and principals relative to the ideal role of the assistant principal, and findings of the research studies and articles presented in the references of the book's chapters. The compendium is not intended to set forth a model of all possible tasks and competencies for the role of the assistant school principal, but should serve the practical purpose of presenting the primary tasks and competencies for the position. The competency-based information in the chapter, in many cases, can be immediately applied to the practices of most school districts. Minor changes and/

or additions to the listings can be made so that they meet a school's program needs. Although the listings of the indicators of competencies are quite comprehensive, you will find many opportunities to add to these listings as fits your school's situation.

Note that in some cases partial illustrations of the assistant principal's tasks and competencies in this chapter were illustrated in previous chapters. Not all of these partial illustrations are included in the comprehensive task, competency and indicators listings in this chapter. Some of the previous illustrations might be appropriate as additions to the following listings.

The information regarding the applications of competency-based administration can help improve administrative practices in your school by:

- Defining specifically the kind(s) of knowledge and skills needed to accomplish the school's mission and indicating how they are demonstrated in the performance of the employee.

- Establishing a framework of knowledge and skills needed to perform the required tasks of the position. In addition, the consideration of indicators of competencies extends the focus to student outcomes.

- Linking the required position competencies to the school's mission, goals and objectives. Facilitating the alignment of all school employees to a single vision of a learning culture.

- Using the position competencies to identify the individual growth and development needs for the assistant principal.

- Establishing purposes related to performance assessment and evaluation requirements; clarifying what performance is expected of the respective school administrators.

- Encouraging the creativity of the assistant principal. Knowing what is to be done in the position opens the door for personal initiative in getting the job done.

- Fostering efficiency in performance by not only defining the tasks of the assistant principal's position and indicating how the tasks can best be achieved but indicating how such achievements are evidenced in the assistant principal's performance.

- Defining the tasks, competencies and indicators of competencies so that administrative performance can be assessed, measured and improved.

- Giving more objectivity to hiring practices. Interviewing procedures are focused on knowledge, skills and the candidate's individual abilities as opposed to subjective judgments that are not directly related to position effectiveness.

- Providing a meaningful relationship between the work of the school principal and the assistant principal. Position responsibilities indicate a division of labor between the principal and assistant principal and provide evidence of a cooperative, supportive relationship.

■ Illustrating to others the paramount importance of the assistant principal's role in the school and helping them to appreciate the beneficial services that you can provide.

A Compendium of Competency-Based Tasks, Competencies, and Indicators of Competencies for the Assistant School Principal

Task

1.0 To function as an instructional leader of the school.

Competency

1.1 Ability to initiate activities to improve instruction and student learning.

Indicators

1.1.1 Understands and implements a variety of methods for instructional improvement.

1.1.2 Interprets and communicates program evaluation results.

1.1.3 Implements school and district goals in all curricular plans.

1.1.4 Conducts internal and external scanning measures to determine school and community educational needs.

1.1.5 Aids in performance evaluations through classroom visitations, reporting observations and evaluating instructional material resources.

Competency

1.2 Ability to establish a learning culture in the school that focuses on student achievement as the primary purpose of the school.

Indicators

1.2.1 Studies and applies the most recent research data relative to how students learn.

1.2.2 Supports staff efforts to determine individual student strengths, interests and instructional needs.

1.2.3 Sets high expectations in regard to student learning outcomes.

1.2.4 Makes clear his/her support of an inclusive school in which all students can learn in the least restricted environment.

Competency

1.3 Ability to assess classroom teaching and student data for the purposes of identifying program strengths and improvement needs.

Indicators

1.3.1 Uses a variety of approaches to assess teaching performance: self-evaluation, 360 degree and peer evaluation methods.

1.3.2 Differentiates formative and summative assessments of personnel classroom performances.

1.3.3 Works cooperatively with teachers in the evaluation of testing results and determining program follow-up changes.

Competency

1.4 Ability to apply knowledge of state standards and district school goals and academic achievement targets.

Indicators

1.4.1 Uses state standards and district and school achievement standards in planning school programs and activities.

1.4.2 Uses state and school achievement standards for assessing academic testing results relative to student gains and gaps between results and existing standards.

Competency

1.5 Ability to analyze achievement data and communicate these results to faculty personnel for the purposes of identifying program strengths and areas in need of improvement.

Indicators

    1.5.1 Seeks and uses available technical resources for calculating testing data and designing charts that illustrate testing outcomes.

    1.5.2 Gives special attention to program strengths and their continuation. Evaluates areas that test below desired standards and works cooperatively with school personnel in determining program changes.

Competency

    1.6 Ability to participate meaningfully in the processes of internal and external scanning relative to the school community program strengths and weaknesses.

Indicators

    1.6.1 Implements both external and internal scanning strategies to determine resource strengths and weaknesses and opportunities and threats for the purpose of guiding all planning efforts.

    1.6.2 Uses internal and external scanning as a tool to avoid strategic surprises and to ensure the continuation of a positive school environment.

Competency

    1.7 Ability to develop a working knowledge of special education curricula and the district's gifted education program.

Indicators

    1.7.1 Becomes actively involved in the (IEP) process with special education curricula and the district gifted and talented programs.

    1.7.2 Works with all faculty personnel in building a school philosophy of inclusion in the regular classroom.

    1.7.3 Follows a personal plan for keeping abreast of effective practices and learning strategies for special needs students.

Competency

    1.8 Ability to stand responsible for student achievement results and establish positive attitudes among all faculty personnel for meeting accountabilities in regard to student achievement.

Indicators

1.8.1 Works to establish a "team culture" on the part of all school personnel in relation to program successes and unsatisfactory program results.

1.8.2 Personally participates in constructive staff development activities relating to special needs student programs.

1.8.3 Gains faculty trust by accepting responsibility for program decisions that do not prove effective. Seeks input from others regarding recommendations for program changes, including best empirical and scientific research results.

1.8.4 Keeps informed about new instructional methods and computer technology and how they might serve to facilitate improvements.

1.8.5 Maintains articulation with feeder schools and institutions of higher education.

1.8.6 Is knowledgeable relative to differences in how students learn and discusses such information with all teaching personnel.

Task

2.0 To function as an effective leader of student activities and organizations.

Competency

2.1 Ability to assume leadership for organizing and administering student activities and organizations.

Indicators

2.1.1 Organizes student activity schedules and oversees the administration of all student organizations including fund accounts in cooperation with other school personnel.

2.1.2 Provides in-service training for faculty sponsors regarding student organizations.

2.1.3 Implements district and school policy and regulations concerning student fund accounts.

2.1.4 Understands and oversees the legal aspects of student activity accounts.

2.1.5 Maintains accurate records of student fund accounts.

2.1.6 Serves as sponsor or liaison for the student council.

2.1.7 Maintains open communication among student organizations, sponsors, and between organizations and the school administration.

Competency

2.2 Ability to organize and supervise the school's sports and intra-mural programs.

Indicators

2.2.1 Supervises and organizes the school's sports and intra-mural programs in cooperation with coaches and intra-mural sponsors.

2.2.2 Manages athletic events including transportation and the enlistment of workers.

2.2.3 Prepares and maintains athletic budgets.

2.2.4 Maintains the athletic programs within all legal requirements and restraints.

2.2.5 Understands and implements state organizations' rules and interscholastic and district policies.

Competency

2.3 Ability to plan facility usage and maintain a master activity schedule.

Indicators

2.3.1 Organizes and publishes the school's activity schedule.

2.3.2 Participates in planning for future facility improvements, changes and additions.

Task

3.0 To function as a school leader in the human resources function of the school.

Competency

3.1 Participates and/or leads in the administration of the primary human resources processes of recruiting, selecting, orienting, assigning, evaluating and in-servicing faculty personnel.

Indicators

3.1.1 Assumes the leadership for determining faculty and support personnel position needs.

3.1.2 Works closely with the school district human resources office in the recruitment process.

3.1.3 Completes the necessary forms and procedures for securing position applicants.

3.1.4 Works with the school staff in designing competency-based interview forms.

3.1.5 Provides in-service training for school interviewers.

3.1.6 Makes hiring decisions on the bases of competency-based position requirements.

3.1.7 Cooperates with teachers and others in implementing an effective orientation program.

3.1.8 Participates with the school principal in administering teacher performance evaluations.

3.1.9 Works with individual school personnel in designing an individual development plan based on a competency-based perspective.

3.1.10 Analyzes performance results for determining recommendations for program and instructional improvements.

3.1.11 Understands the different purposes of formative and summative evaluations.

Competency

3.2 Ability to determine, organize, and administer effective professional growth and development programs and activities.

Indicators

3.2.1 Uses performance testing and research data for organizing professional growth and development activities.

3.2.2 Is a consumer, disseminater and utilizer of educational research relating to adult learning and best practices for performance improvement.

3.2.3 Plans and participates in a personal growth and development program on an ongoing basis.

Task

4.0 To foster and main positive relationships with members of the school community.

Competency

4.1 Ability to maintain effective relationships with all facets of the school community.

Indicators

4.1.1 Maintains effective relations with members of the school community by establishing means for the community to participate in school program planning and development.

4.1.2 Is involved in community programs and activities.

4.1.3 Implements communication strategies whereby parents and other community members can express their concerns regarding school matters.

4.1.4 Encourages members of the community to utilize school facilities.

4.1.5 Assesses and utilizes community resources to assist in determining school goals and objectives.

4.1.6 Joins community organizations for the primary purpose of contributing to the betterment of the community of residence.

Competency

4.2 Ability to work effectively with the media.

Indicators

4.2.1 Knows the persons in the media and takes steps to learn about the newspapers, radio stations, and TV stations in the school community.

4.2.2 Assumes co-leadership with the principal for the school's public relations program.

4.2.3 Works cooperatively with the school principal, teachers, and district director of community affairs in planning and programming public relations information for parents and the school community.

4.2.4 Administers periodic parental surveys that center on gaining their opinions on school matters and requesting their evaluations of ongoing school programs.

4.2.5 Works with the community media in organizing and conducting school marketing programs.

4.2.6 Responds promptly when the school is contacted by the press by answering questions posed or referring the press to the appropriate person.

4.2.7 Understands that nothing is "off the record."

4.2.8 Understands that school reports and surveys are public property. Does not withhold such information but knows that the law does protect the privacy of personal information about students and staff.

4.2.9 Understands that the school district media relations director is the individual responsible for the school district's public relations program.

Task

5.0 To function as the school's co-leader of the human resources function.

Competency

5.1 Ability to plan and provide leadership for the administration of student personnel services and procedures for developing and maintaining a high level of student behavior.

Indicators

5.1.1 Supervises academic placement for guidance personnel to direct students into the most appropriate classes, programs and activities.

5.1.2 Works closely with special programs, including special education, vocational education and gifted student programs, to ensure that such programs are on-target for meeting student needs.

5.1.3 Manages and supervises the school's attendance procedures.

5.1.4 Supervises the entirety of attendance operations from implementing school board policy to the computation of average daily attendance.

5.1.5 Maintains a system by which teachers and parents are informed of student tardiness and absences.

5.1.6 Demonstrates an understanding of legal aspects of state and district attendance laws and policies by implementing them in school rules and administrative decisions.

5.1.7 Develops procedures and activities to improve student absenteeism and tardiness.

5.1.8 Serves in the selection, supervision, assistance and evaluation of classified personnel.

5.1.9 Consciously works to keep open the channels of communication with the teaching staff.

Task

6.0 To foster a positive learning environment in the school.

Competency

6.1 Ability to create a safe school environment for students and the school personnel including student behavior.

Indicators

6.1.1 Checks safety measures in the school such as fire alarms and extinguishers and safety hazards in the school and on the campus.

6.1.2 Works with others to complete a procedures booklet for dealing with emergencies such as bomb threats, intruders, and gun threats.

6.1.3 Holds ongoing sessions with the professional and support personnel regarding school safety, nurse's office, cafeteria services, transportation services, and extra-curricular programs to provide needed support for these student services.

6.1.4 Takes actions to implement a positive approach to student discipline.

6.1.5 Places an emphasis on dealing with discipline as a teaching and learning opportunity.

6.1.6 Learns about research findings concerning various discipline practices.

6.1.7 Maintains accurate records of student discipline cases and the results of actions taken.

6.1.8 Initiates preventive measures that serve to reduce discipline problems and keep students in the school's learning environment.

6.1.9 Updates the school's student handbook relative to discipline and leads information sessions on the topic with students new to the school.

6.1.10 Assesses school plant and equipment needs and requests resources for maintenance and repair of the school plant with strict attention to safety measures.

6.1.11 Establishes a close working relationship with the law enforcement offices that relate to the school.

6.1.12 Demonstrates the traits of a student advocate in respect to student rights, student special interests and needs, inclusiveness, fairness, and communication.

6.1.13 Administers student climate surveys and gives due consideration to the survey results.

Task

7.0 To accept management responsibilities for the general operations of the school.

Competency

7.1 Ability to exercise responsibilities for the development and/or completion of reports, records, and written communications desired or required to facilitate the work of the school and school district.

Indicators

7.1.1 Manages, prioritizes and performs important responsibilities including the development and completion of reports, records, and written communication desired or required to facilitate the work of the school and school district.

7.1.2 Manages the school building and school district physical plant to ensure maximum usage and safe conditions.

7.1.3 Works closely with the spectrum of the regional accrediting agencies.

Competency

7.2 Ability to prepare the budget and control budget expenditures.

Indicators

7.2.1 Prepares the budget for the school areas of student activities.

7.2.2 Budgets for the maintenance, alterations and needed improvements of the school plant.

7.2.3 Monitors spending so that all seasonal activities have parity of available funds.

7.2.4 Maintains income and expenditure account records for all student service accounts and school maintenance requirements.

Competency

7.3 Ability to perform duties of the principal when necessary.

Indicators

7.3.1 Has a general knowledge of the duties and responsibilities of the principal.

7.3.2 Makes necessary decisions fairly and decisively.

7.3.3 Performs as co-leader of the school in other management tasks as requested by the school principal.

Competency

7.4 Ability to understand the differences and relationships among district board policies, administrative regulations and local school rules and how each applies in practice.

Indicators

7.4.1 Uses school board policy as a guideline to work with the school district and school principal to develop relevant administrative regulations for the school district.

7.4.2 Cooperates with the school principal and members of the school faculty in developing important school rules to guide student procedures relating to safety, attendance, behavior, scholarship and other school operations.

7.4.3 Disseminates school rules to students and parents by completing and distributing a student handbook with follow-up confirmation that the handbook was received.

Task

8.0 To exercise proper management of the school for planned as well as unplanned/routine daily operations.

Competency

    8.1 Ability to manage time, define and prioritize responsibilities related to the position description approved by the school principal and school district.

Indicators

    8.1.1 Follows the required list of tasks and competencies set forth in the position description.

    8.1.2 Has a procedure for determining task priorities and completes duties in priority order and within the limits of a time line. Determines those things that are important and urgent, important but not urgent, important but can wait, busy work/wasted time.

    8.1.3 Demonstrates administrative flexibility by taking care of emergency measures as they arise.

    8.1.4 Communicates with the school principal periodically relative to priority changes that should be considered.

    8.1.5 Demonstrates an understanding of time management by creating time line strategies for each task/responsibility on the priority list.

    8.1.6 Implements a self-assessment strategy that centers on keeping a log of activities of the week. Asks: What went well and why? What did not go well and why not? What needs to be changed in my behavior?

    8.1.7 Uses strategies that buffer himself/herself from interruptions.

Competency

    8.2 Ability to organize, coordinate and delegate authority.

Indicators

    8.2.1 Understands and utilizes the delegation of authority. Uses teacher leaders wisely.

    8.2.2 Understands and accepts the scope of authority.

    8.2.3 Works to build a learning school environment that focuses on design, teaching and stewardship where school personnel have opportunities to continually expand their capabilities.

    8.2.4 Shares the leadership and assumes the responsibility for developing a school mission that focuses on a shared purpose of cooperation directed to the continuous improvement of student learning.

8.2.5 Understands the differences and relationships between school policy, administrative regulations and school rules. Works professionally to promote policies and regulations that promote the best interests of students.

Using the Competency-Based Compendium to Create a Position Application Form for a Fourth Grade Teacher

In the following section the practical use of the foregoing competency-based compendium is illustrated in creating a position application form for a fourth grade teaching position (see Box 6.1). The school is one of ten elementary schools in the district and has an enrollment of 354 students in grades K–6. It might appear rather simplistic to include an application form in this chapter. However, the purpose is to illustrate the connection between competency-based posting of a school position and the follow-up interview and selection processes.

Box 6.1 Position Application for a Teaching Position

Position Application

Bethany School District
Havelock Elementary School
Fourth grade teacher

The position: Havelock Elementary School is seeking a qualified candidate to fill a fourth grade teaching position. Havelock Elementary School has an enrollment of 354 students. The average pupil teacher ratio is 25 to 1. Havelock is rated as a high performance school and rated "A" relative to students' annual improvement.

Responsible to: The assistant principal and principal of Havelock Elementary School

Primary Position Tasks

1. To function as an instructional leader in the classroom.

2. To establish and maintain appropriate standards for student behavior.

3. To establish positive relationships with parents.

4. To create a positive environment in the classroom conducive to student learning.

5. To maintain professional competence by participating in a planned program for continuous performance improvement.

6. To administer required group standardized tests in accordance with state and school board standards.

7. To participate in school district and school faculty curriculum development activities.

8. To supervise students in extra-curricular activities and in the school throughout the day.

Primary Competencies Required

1. Ability to teach reading, language arts, social studies, mathematics, science, art, health and music to students in the classroom using the approved school district's course of study.

2. Ability to determine the student's success level for learning and provide appropriate instruction for academic improvement.

3. Ability to develop appropriate daily lesson plans and materials that serve individual students.

4. Ability to use a variety of instructional methods/strategies to meet the learning styles of each student.

5. Ability to assess and evaluate the student's academic and social growth, keeps appropriate records and maintains progress data reports.

6. Ability to communicate with parents through personal contacts, conferences and other means to gain input and provide recommendations.

7. Ability to plan and develop an individual development plan in cooperation with the assistant principal.

8. Ability to work with the assistant school principal in developing a performance evaluation plan in accordance with state and school district standards.

9. Ability to implement discipline procedure that centers on a learning outcome.

Credentials Required

a. Bachelor's degree in elementary education from an accredited college or university.

b. Appropriate state teaching certificate.

c. Must complete a background check.

d. Original copy of college/university transcripts.

e. Names and positions of three to five references.

Teacher Application[1]

1. Applicant's name and address including best contact methods (e.g., phone, email address and best times to contact the applicant.)

2. Position desired: The specific position openings would be listed here with an entry indicating availability (e.g., full time, part time, substitute). Request activities that the applicant would be qualified to direct, sponsor, or coach.

3. Professional qualifications regarding degrees held, date received and institution issuing the degrees.

    Entry for major, minor and bachelor's and graduate grade point averages.

    Teaching certificate held and state of issue, kind of certification, level, and date for renewal.

    Listing of teaching experience with name of school, grade/subjects and dates. Listing of other professional work experience to be included.

4. Employment history: Start by listing the most current or most recent employer and extend history for at least 10 years.

    For each employer list the position, dates of employment, address of employment, supervisor's name and contact information with appropriate authorizations to contact these employers in regard to the applicant's work record. Specify the related competencies needed to fulfill each position.

    List the names, positions, addresses of three to five references who are qualified to speak of your personal traits and professional competencies with appropriate authorizations to contact these references in regard to the applicant's work record.

5. Descriptions of other relevant information such as military service, personal accomplishments, recognitions and/or awards received, and so forth commonly are included in application forms.

    Approval to conduct a background check is needed as well.

6. The approval to do a background check and to ask specific questions relative to the applicant's criminal record and reasons for leaving prior positions are included in some position applications depending on state laws and school board policies.

Note: [1] Note that the teacher application form will not be detailed here. Rather, the primary information that is to be completed by the applicant is noted with major sections that commonly would be included along with a brief description of the kinds of information to be completed in that particular section.

Position Analysis and Position Descriptions

Hiring history has revealed that 50 percent of the teachers hired each year by your school will not be on the staff after five years. This is just the way it is in education, right? We do not think this needs to be so. If the hiring and retention of faculty and staff personnel are to be improved, much more needs to be done to change the situation. Without your administrative leadership this goal will not be accomplished. We submit that improvement falls short of the desired goals when it centers primarily on current practices that have not been too successful in the first place. Both empirical and scientific research have found that certain education practices are flawed yet continue to be implemented. One example centers on the practice of failing students in grade. A volume of studies has found that such a practice does more damage than good in regard to student learning. Education has been negligent in implementing certain human resources procedures as well. Few school districts have implemented the administration of position analysis as part of the hiring process. Schools want and need better hiring "fits" but few have initiated the strategy of position analyses for developing position descriptions for either professional or support personnel.

Position Analysis and Its Implications for Improving Position Descriptions of All Personnel

We believe that it is important to explain why the topic of position analysis is important in a book centering on the work of the assistant school principal. After all, not many schools or even school districts complete position analyses activities for professional teachers. There are at least three basic reasons that illustrate why specific knowledge about position analysis and position description relate directly to the work of contemporary administration at the local school level.

There is a current need to gain a better knowledge and understanding of human resources administration at all levels of schooling today. Just assuming that all teachers at all levels and in different subject areas do the same job falls short of reality. Improvement of academic performance on the part of teachers is a headline topic in education today. In regard to teaching, however, just what aspects of teaching are most problematic and in need of primary attention is not clear. Merely asking for improved student achievement is not sufficient to provide a focused improvement perspective.

Class size has received considerable attention in relation to inhibiting student learning. Yet, we know of few schools that have considered teacher load on a scientific, objective basis. Although objective measures of teacher load have been available for more than fifty years, their applications in practice have been limited at best. As a result, teacher workload assignments differ at the secondary school levels and the load of some teachers is three times that of teachers with the lightest workloads. As a result, the best teachers in the school commonly have the greatest workloads and in the long run their teaching can be reduced to a level of actual mediocrity. Work responsibilities for teachers are constantly changing. In fact, there need to be some methods to assess these changes and reach decisions about work positions on a fair and equitable basis. Just saying that each teacher will teach five out of six class periods a day or four out of five class periods leaves ample opportunities for inequalities of load to exist.

We believe that there is no position in your school today that is so well established that it does not lend itself to improvement. When properly conceived and actually administered, position analysis can serve as a primary vehicle for improving the structure and effectiveness of teaching as well as the work of administrative and support personnel. Administrative personnel in schools who have anything to do with the personnel function should know and understand four job related terms: "A **position analysis** is the process of examining the contents of a position and breaking it down into its significant tasks. It is a scientific, in-depth analysis of the position and includes its constituent parts and surrounding environment" (Norton, 2008, p. 112). A **position description** evolves from a position analysis and consists of a written statement of facts pertaining to the position in question. Commonly, the position description includes the job title, general tasks and responsibilities, specific competencies, and position qualifications. **Job grading** is the ranking of jobs used primarily for classified staff positions, although salary schedules for the professional staff are indicative of job grading as well. **Job assessment** is the ascription of a monetary value for a job on the basis of job grading. As noted, teacher's salary schedules are a form of job assessment based on preparation and experience (Norton, 2008).

Since the completion of a position analysis for a specific subject area takes considerable time, when funds permit, an outside consultant is hired to do the analysis. Nevertheless, we submit that money used for beneficial purposes tends to more than save expenditures over the long run. In other instances, the central human resources office of the school district can serve in the administration of position analyses. With proper study of position analysis purposes and procedures, it is quite possible that the assistant principal and principal could complete this work satisfactorily over time. Time spent on position analysis could account for itself in time saving on problems relating to poor hires, ineffective in-service activities and performance assessments. Using valid data to improve teaching programs is an accepted practice today. We submit that valid data regarding work conditions and load equities can serve the educational services of our schools as well.

You need to note just how the work to complete position analyses for your school's employees pays off. Here's how you, the school and the school district benefit by the process.

Benefits of a position analysis

1. Provides a position focus relative to the goals of the school and school system; ties the position strategically to these goals. In addition, it serves as the basis for role examination and learning just how the position effects the mental and physical conditions of the employee.

2. Provides a realistic basis for evaluating the job itself and suggests ways for improving the conditions of the position and employee performance needs.

3. Serves as a basis for recruiting and ultimately selecting both certificated and classified personnel; pinpoints position qualifications and fosters the possibility of best fit for the position at hand.

4. Serves as the basis for planning and implementing a relevant employee development program.

5. Provides the information needed to draft a relevant position description and a legal statement for the school and school district relative to questions about hiring, performance assessment/evaluation, and dismissal.

The Position Analysis and Its Common Contents

A position analysis commonly contains seven content areas. Box 6.2 sets forth these common content areas and Box 6.3 is an illustration of the first three content areas of a mathematics teacher's position analysis. Although the information is gathered through the use of Box 6.2, additional entries relative to the nature of the position and employee qualifications would be appropriate.

It should be noted that the printed position analysis form for each specific grade and/or subject matter is completed by the employees in those areas. The results of all employees' responses are recorded. In turn, the grade level chairs, supervisors or assistant principal critically review the responses and recommend changes they see as necessary. Major differences between the employees' entries and their supervisors are reconciled through face-to-face meetings. The result is one of the primary benefits of doing a position analysis; the parties end up agreeing as to what the position(s) really entails, including outcome production results.

Box 6.2 Common Content Areas for a Position Analysis

The Nature of the Position

The general description of the position
The materials, equipment and technology used in the position
The time requirements for completing the required tasks
Expectations of work outcomes, including goals and objectives, standards of
    output
The work environment including employee relationships
Permanent, temporary, periodic work position
The coordination of the flow of work

The Necessary Employee Qualifications

The special tasks and competencies required of the employee
The required licenses, certifications and experience required for the position
Work experience required or preferred
Knowledge required in the position
Nature of standardized practices for carrying out the work
Language requirements including oral and written communication
Special technological skills required

The Work Environment and Effects on the Employee

The physical and mental effects on the worker such as stress, safety, peer
    relationships, supervisory relationships, health, work-life balance, turnover
Special abilities required in the position
Day, evening, night work schedules, indoor, outdoor
Experience requirements
Absence and lateness records
Physical requirements related to standing/sitting, lifting, walking and stability
Independent or dependent work relationships
Primary problems and position inhibitors

The Relationship of the Position to the School System

How the position is supervised
Supervision given by the employee
Line and staff relationships
Available support services utilized
Guidance given by school federal and state laws and school board policies
Reporting requirements

Performance Evaluation Activities
Program, school and school district coordination

The Relationship of the Position to the School Community

Parental relationships and communication requirements
Cooperative partnerships with community agencies
Support agencies within the school community
Public pressures, parental demands
School politics

Box 6.3 An Example of a Position Analysis Form for a Middle School Mathematics Teacher

Job Analysis Questionnaire

Directions: This is to request your help in furnishing information for the development of your job description and a job classification system for your job family. Please answer and/or describe as best you can the characteristics and factors of your job and the job qualifications as requested in each of the following entries.

1. In this section, the employee's name and location, immediate supervisor, and other contact information is detailed.

2. JOB DESCRIPTION: In this section, the position title, length of work year, present salary, official position title, full-time/part-time, and a listing of the *most important tasks of the position* are to be listed.

3. What are the additional tasks and responsibilities of this job that must be performed?

4. Describe the physical conditions under which you work and any unusual situations: such as interruptions, noise, confusion, disturbances, etc.

5. Is it necessary for you to handle sums of money as a responsibility of this job? Please explain.

6. How many people do you supervise, if any? Please list them, but exclude students.

7. Identify the skills and knowledge that are necessary for serving satisfactorily in this position (e.g., typing a certain number of words per minute, ability to repair school appliances, ability to read blueprints, ability to prepare a variety of foods for students, etc.).

8. List the types of equipment that you must be able to operate in your job. Please be specific and all-inclusive in your listing.

9. Please identify the contacts that you believe best represent the human relations contacts of your job. Explain as best you can the nature of the contacts/communications of major importance.

10. The nature of your work demands what type of activity: such as sitting, standing, walking, climbing, carrying, etc.?

11. List four of your job's most important activities and the approximate percentage of time that you must spend with each one.

12. To what extent are you responsible for your own work? That is, do you determine primarily what you are to do; or is part of what you do assigned by another person; or is your work primarily given to you by another person?

13. What license or certificate is required for you to hold? In your opinion, what grade level is required to perform the tasks required of your job?

14. List your personal information concerning what growth and development requirements you have been required to meet to hold the position. List the licenses and certificates that you do hold.

15. List the present grade of your job. In your opinion, is this grade classification for your position a correct one?

16. Please list your educational history (grade completion, college work, business/vocational schools, other).

17. List the previous work experiences that you have had and give the approximate dates for this experience.

18. List the kinds of supervision that you might provide in your present position. In addition, give some indication of the nature of this supervisory responsibility (e.g., work assignments, performance evaluations, orientation of new workers, service as a mentor or coach, etc.).

Your signature _____ Date _____

Toward Equity in Workload Assignments for Elementary and Secondary Teachers

We previously mentioned that teacher load inequities tend to militate against quality performances by our best teachers. We commonly assign difficult tasks to our most competent employees since we know that they will do their best to get the job done. Yet, over time, this practice limits the teacher's time and energy and it affects classroom teaching in a negative way. "Maximization of human resources is inhibited seriously if inequitable distribution of load exists, or if load is unwisely allocated" (Norton, 2008, p. 168). In addition, research studies have found that many teachers with the lowest teacher load indices commonly complain about their heavy workload. We noted previously that personnel who are most qualified to carry out an effective educational program in the school often are so overburdened that their efforts are forced to a level of actual mediocrity. "Inequitable and burdensome workload militates against quality teacher performance and the stability of teachers in the profession" (Norton, 2008, p. 172).

When teachers are asked about their workload, they often respond by indicating the number of subjects that they teach per day. Some would mention class size as well. However, there are other factors that are present in teacher load, including the subject taught, the grade level of the subject, the length of class periods, the number of class preparations required, and time spent on cooperative duty assignments.

Work satisfaction for employees is a goal of every school administrator. How would an assistant principal benefit by implementing a valid measure of every teacher's workload? First and foremost is the fact that the results of a valid measure of workload provide data that allow you to compare work assignments and adjust them equitably. It provides information that allows the administrative staff to examine carefully the workload of teachers new to the school and possibly serves as a positive retention tool.

Workload data give you a valid basis for assigning classes and cooperative duties to the teaching faculty. As human beings, teachers might argue that their own workload is much higher than that of others, but can readily understand statistical findings that are based on objective measures for all teachers.

Objective load measurements provide hard data for illustrating the need for additional faculty personnel. And, as previously mentioned, teacher load measurement results quickly reveal inequities in workload assignments. This can have an impact on the job satisfaction of your entire staff. "Such data loom important in accounting for the work contributions of the teaching staff relative to both in-class and extracurricular responsibilities" (Norton, 2008, p. 168). Such measurement instruments as the Douglass Secondary Teacher Load Formula (1951) and the Norton/Bria Elementary Teacher Load Formula (1992) can be valuable tools for gaining equity in teacher workload assignments.

An Application of the Competency-Based Concept in Relation to Time Management

The topic of time management has been of concern historically and remains so today. If a person wants tips on managing time it is only necessary to use the web and find more suggestions than can realistically be implemented. Few of them are actually helpful, however. Here are a few jewels that were suggested in several different time management tip articles: Prepare yourself first, by taking 30 minutes of your time to fix yourself something to eat and relax. Take a break, clear your mind and refresh yourself to refocus. Leave time for fun. Know yourself. Get it done, the sooner the better. Strive to be authentic. Maintain a life style that will give you maximum energy. Spot trouble ahead and solve problems immediately. Differentiate between urgent and important tasks; an urgent task may not necessarily be important. Before you can even begin to manage time, you must learn what time is. Identify areas of your life where you are wasting time and try to reduce these. Keep a diary of what things you have done and do them more quickly next time. People who have achieved the most have made the most mistakes. Never leave till tomorrow what you can do today. Time flies or drags depending on what you're doing. To create time and space for critical priorities, one must first of all be clear about what they and their teams will stop doing. Step one—identify five things—no more—that you want to focus on for the year and spend 95 percent of your time on those things. Use to-do lists to manage your employees more closely. Keep in mind that there just isn't enough time to get all the things done that you want to do. Work smarter instead of harder. Stop wasting your time. Just say NO.

Well, that does it—or does it? The very least you could do is to implement the very first tip in the list, "Prepare yourself first, by taking 30 minutes of your time to fix yourself something to eat and relax." We will move on with the topic of time management by implementing the concept of competency.

The Human Resources Systems Group Ltd. (HRSG) makes a key point that serves the purposes of this chapter. As stated by HRSG (2013), "Organizations improve efficiency not only as employees learn 'what' they are expected to do, but even more as they understand 'how' to perform tasks" (p. 1). As noted by the primary goal of this chapter, competency-based performance sets forth the primary tasks of responsibility and the guidelines for understanding how to achieve them successfully.

Two primary functions of all school administrators are planning and organization. In this section, we concentrate on these administrative functions and relate them to the ever present need for time management. The importance of effective planning rests in the fact that planning sets the foundation for all other administrative functions. More than 100 years ago, Taylor (1911) included the task of planning as one of four primary concepts of his task system. In Taylor's system, however, management had the responsibility to plan work and control its accomplishment.

"Without planning there can be little intelligent direction for activity . . . Planning is an essential component of the administrative process" (Campbell & Gregg, 1957, p. 281). Effective planning and organizing ultimately are the end products of the school leader's administrative skills and the results of hard work. Planning is important because it offsets uncertainty and fosters positive change. It serves to focus on important goals and objectives and can result in a more effective organizational operation.

Planning is essential for determining what decisions, programs, activities, and resources you will need to achieve the right results. Effective planning serves to identify the goals that your school is to achieve; it fosters effective administration and promotes optimal work performance on your part as well as the school staff. More than forty years ago, Koontz and O'Donnell (1972) defined planning as "deciding in advance what to do, when to do it, and who is to do it. Planning bridges the gap from where we are to where we want to go" (p. 113). One thing seems certain, for you to be successful in the demanding role of assistant principal, you will have to be a competent planner.

What Planning Is Not

In an attempt to define planning, sometimes it helps to explain what it is not. First of all, planning is not the same as the plan itself. **Planning** is an ongoing process that is continuous, flexible and subject to change. A **plan** is a product of the planning process; it is time- and place-specific. Good planning is not an after-school brainstorming session that is merely a reaction to immediate needs and concerns. It is not simply the organizing of certain committees that will report back their ideas on one particular problem or program provision. It is not the establishment of the school or school system's vision without the follow-up procedures for implementing specific goals and objectives and administering and evaluating the goals and objectives set forth. Nor is the plan a public relations announcement that the school is completing a year-long study of programs and operations that seem to fade away until it's time to do another study.

Perhaps Young (2008) said it best: "Planning is a methodological mechanism for projecting intentions and actions rather than reacting to causes and events impacting the schooling process" (p. 62). The process that serves to determine what policy decisions, programs, activities, and resources are necessary to achieve the desired results is termed **strategy** (Norton, 2008, p. 102). Strategic planning, properly implemented, can be a dynamic process for helping you achieve positive changes that lead to an improved school future.

Does the Way We Plan Determine the Way We Organize?

It is not uncommon to think of the term "organization" as a physical structure, or as one school superintendent once said, "I think of organization as a clean desk." Rather "organizations are the coordination of different activities of individual contributors to carry out planned transactions within the environment" (Laurence & Lorsch, 1967). A school system in reality, like any other organization, is complex and often ambiguous. It seems that all too often we wonder just what is going on up there. The challenge for you as an assistant principal is to learn to deal with this complexity. If you don't build this capacity you most likely will never have the ability to find new ways of performing your responsibilities and solving the problems that you encounter on a daily basis.

The authorities tell us that the way we design an organization shapes both the input and output of what we do, controls our purposes, inhibits or fosters creativity and mandates the style of authority that will prevail. For example, as Morgan (1987) has pointed out, if the organization is designed and operated as if it were a machine, we get a rationalistic, mechanistic result. Control is placed in the hands of central office personnel and policies and regulations, mission statements, position descriptions and performance evaluations are implemented to keep the machine operational.

On the other hand, such things as necessary change, initiative, self-determined growth, flexibility and diverse thinking are facilitated in what Morgan terms a holographic: the ability of organizations to self-organize. That is, the capacities to hold the organization together are enfolded in all its parts. If one part fails or is removed, other parts take over and self-reorganization takes place. Or what if we designed schools and school districts as heterarchial organizations whereby the dominant element depended on the situation at hand? In this type of organization, employee roles are allowed to change and evolve according to the circumstances. Different people take the initiative on different occasions according to the contribution they are able to make to the task at hand. Inquiry rather than pre-design provides the main driving force.

Our purpose in this discussion of organization models is not to prescribe or support them, but rather to underscore the fact that how we organize directly affects what we do administratively. So it does seem reasonable that if you do not like the outcomes of your program activities, organizational changes appear to be in order.

Hanlon (1968) spoke of the most difficult but important part of planning: conceptualizing the plan of work. He used the idea of artist Leonardo da Vinci "that the execution of the work of art is the easiest part of the artist's job, while the most difficult part is the conception and composition of that work" (p. 29). It makes little difference what strokes of the artist's brush are used without the conception and plan because none results in a better painting than any other. Hanlon underscores the crux of this point by noting that the conception of the plan and the plan itself provide the guidelines for assessing the decisions and activities of the personnel in the organization in terms of what they envision the organization to be in the future. When your school personnel have a limited conception of the school's plan, they are deciding and acting without guidelines for achieving the desired results. But keep clearly in mind that the plaque on the school wall with its brief mission statement is just that, a written statement. Unless you work to identify the employees' tasks and the competencies needed to accomplish them, the outcomes will be no better than any others.

How Strategic Planning Can Serve You Well

Some authorities argue that merely attempting to prepare for the future falls short of the desired ends. Rather, as Pfeiffer et al. (1986) point out, the process of strategic planning enables the organization to help change its own future as opposed to simply preparing for future needs and changes. We need to consider strategic planning because the economic conditions, learner needs and expectations, and many other environmental factors that you face now will not be the same in two, five or ten years' time. Strategic planning is not necessarily the making of future decisions; rather it is focused upon the current planning decisions of what should be done now to realize desired outcomes in the future. Strategic planning will help you deal with the inevitability of change; it encourages the implementation of effective administration.

Baird et al. (1983) have set seven basic elements required in your strategic plan: (1) The educational environment of the school. An internal and external scan of the school's environment and its culture is needed to determine the many considerations that can be viewed simultaneously as constraints and opportunities. (2) A mission statement that serves to develop a clear vision of the priority goals and objectives that guide the work of your school's personnel. (3) The development and implementation of the school's strategic plan and tying it to the school district's strategic plan in terms of budgeting, curriculum, personnel, and pupil services. (4) Monitoring the effectiveness of the strategic plan on a continuous basis. (5) Examining, analyzing and assessing the results of the school's strategic plan after it is implemented. (6) Determining the gap between assessed results and expected outcomes. (7) Determining needed procedural changes to close the determined outcome gaps.

As Goetz (1949) pointed out more than fifty years ago, administrative actions that are not based on effective planning most likely will result in chaos. So, as a school administrator, you can either work to become competent in planning or spend the time trying to solve the many problems that result.

You obviously cannot carry out such planning alone. The school principal, other school leaders and members of the school staff must have the opportunity to participate. This is what is referred to as participation, collaboration and team building. If this isn't the case, the results of any plan will typically quickly fade into the recesses of the people's minds and gather dust on the desks of faculty members.

Time Management and Competency-Based Solutions for Assistant Principals

In the following section, we consider the major task of achieving a viable procedure for implementing a time management strategy through the use of a competency-based procedure.

Task

1.0 To implement a time management procedure that benefits the assistant principal and the school.

Competencies

1.1 Ability to control the time available for completing position responsibilities effectively.

Indicators

1.1.1 Takes time to plan and prioritize work responsibilities at the very outset.

1.1.2 Gives careful consideration to work responsibilities and their time requirements in relation to their priority, available resources, personnel support and potential inhibitors.

1.1.3 Maintains a calendar of due dates for work completion; adjusts the schedule as needed periodically.

1.1.4 Establishes a realistic work schedule in terms of due dates: today, tomorrow, this week, next week, the first of next month.

1.1.5 Implements strategies for dealing with inevitable interruptions.

1.1.6 Carries out the time schedule and stays on track by using a time log, cutting telephone calls and conversations and assessing progress on a daily basis.

1.1.7 Gives attention to time requirements when program and activity changes are being considered.

1.2.1 Ability to use teacher leaders, parents and others in the completion of position responsibilities.

1.2.2 Identifies talent within the school to cooperate in the completion of work responsibilities (budget matters, personnel matters, community relations, instructional improvement, setting standards, student services and others).

1.2.3 Uses community support services for administering position responsibilities (health services, student activities, safety practices, personnel development, budget matters, and others).

1.2.4 Uses technology such as an electronic calendar to send out messages to members of the staff regarding progress and target dates.

1.2.5 Avoids procrastination by taking action according to the planned time schedule. Keeps focused on what needs to be done.

1.2.6 Knows the true interests and talents of school personnel and considers these traits in assigning them to work activities.

1.2.7 Understands that ongoing assessments of time management by reviewing master calendars in regard to activities and meetings that are supporting the strategic goals of the school.

We will close the discussion on time management by listing several tips that appear worthy of your consideration (Matthews et al., 2014). Even these writers have little confidence regarding the effectiveness of time management techniques.

As these writers contend, "Everything you ever learned about managing time is a complete waste of time because it doesn't work" (Matthews et al., 2014, p. 1).

Nevertheless several of their suggestions appear to have some merit. Selected suggestions by Matthews and others are as follows (2014, p. 2).

1. Carry a schedule and record all your thoughts, conversations and activities for a week. This will help you understand how much you get done during the course of a day and where your precious moments are going. You'll see how much time is wasted on unproductive thoughts, conversations and actions.

2. Take the first 30 minutes of every day to plan your day. Don't start your day until you complete your time plan. The most important time of your day is the time you schedule to schedule time.

3. Put up a "Do not disturb" sign when you absolutely have to get a work priority done.

4. Practice not answering the phone just because it's ringing or e-mails just because they show up. Instead schedule a time to answer phone calls and return e-mails.

5. Any activity or conversation that's important to your success should have a time assigned to it. To-do lists get longer and longer to the point where they're unworkable. Appointment books work. Schedule appointments with yourself and create time blocks for high-priority thoughts, conversations and actions. Schedule when they begin and end. Have the discipline to keep these appointments.

A Lightbulb Experience

The number 1 entry in the foregoing listing does have merit. Although somewhat tedious, keeping a detailed log of the minutes you spend during one week will be an eye-opener for you. You might argue that you certainly know what you do each week, but if you do the task diligently for one week, I assure you that you will be completely surprised with the results. Just list four or five headings such as meetings, office work, classroom visits, student matters, phone calls, social events or other major areas of your work responsibilities. *Keep an accurate record of events/activities* in each of the major areas as they take place and record the event and the minutes spent. For example, curriculum meeting, 1 hr. 30 min.; parent/student conference, 30 min.; classroom observation, 45 min; candidate interview, 30 min., etc. At the end of the week, add the time spent in each area. How and where are you spending the majority of your time? Is the proportion of time spent in each work area directly related to your position work priorities?

The key, of course, is completing this activity with responsible accuracy. The analysis of time results will present needed changes in terms of your time management. You might learn that your time is being spent on those activities that you prefer to do or ones that are near the bottom of your real priorities.

Effective time management ties closely to many of the concepts discussed in this chapter. Planning and organization lead this consideration. But have you ever given thought to the factors that are your leading time waster? Alec Mackenzie, a leading time management consultant, lists the leading time wasters as experienced by managers of fifteen countries (*U.S. News and World Report*, December 3, 1973, p. 45). Perhaps you could add others to the list that are time wasters for you. Ten selected time wasters noted by MacKenzie were as follows:

1. Telephone interruptions
2. Visitors dropping in without appointments
3. Meetings both scheduled and unscheduled
4. Lack of objectives, priorities and deadlines
5. Cluttered desk and personal disorganization
6. Involvement in routine and detail that should be delegated to others
7. Failure to set up clear lines of responsibility and authority
8. Indecision and procrastination
9. Inability to say "No"
10. Lack of standards and progress reports that enable a manager to keep track of developments.

Our recommendation is that you select one or two of the foregoing time wasters that relate to your situation. For each one, list two or three actions that you will take to remedy the problem. Enforce the actions that you determine. When you find that the first two selections have proven beneficial, choose one or two more and set forth actions that you will take to improve your management of time.

Summary

In order to upgrade the position of assistant school principal, it will be necessary to tie it closely to the important purposes for which the school exists. This chapter is based on the contention that competency-based strategies have much to contribute in realizing this result. As underscored in Chapter 1, the position of assistant principal all too often has been relegated to a position of ill-defined responsibilities that commonly are far removed from the primary purposes and major priorities of effective schools today.

Competency-based programming holds many implications for improving the administrative contributions of the assistant principal to the primary purposes of the school. Chapter 6 presented a compendium of competency-based tasks, competencies and indicators of competencies for assistant principals. Specific ways in which competency-based concepts can enhance the quality of practices in personnel services, student services and other administration functions were discussed.

The need to improve employee hiring practices was presented with competency-based strategies for posting position openings, and dealing with position analysis, position descriptions, position grading and position assessment were detailed.

The paramount importance of planning and organization, including strategic planning and time management, were viewed as being essential for building effective programs in every major administrative function of the school. Planning not only serves as the foundation for building successful school programs but also ties directly to the kind of organization that will evolve in the school.

Time management looms important for assistant principals. This chapter's recommendations for upgrading the position and making it administratively essential will require many new responsibilities and professional development activities that necessitate the ability to manage time effectively. Although absolute solutions to managing time appear to be too evasive, the chapter does present some beneficial recommendations and also considers the concept of time management in terms of a competency-based phenomenon.

Discussion Questions

1. Quickly review the chapter's information regarding the many applications of competency-based administration. After reviewing the suggested applications of the strategy, list one or more other possible applications of competency-based administration at the assistant school principal's level.

2. Think about the terms job grading and job assessment. Write down their definitions and then apply them to such activities as classified personnel pay schedules. How are these terms evident commonly in the salary schedules of the teaching faculty?

3. Assume that you just conducted a walk-through classroom observation of a high school social studies teacher. Your walk-through checklist listed "evidence of student participation." You checked that entry as "not observed". In your feedback to the teacher, list two or three competencies that you might recommend for his/her consideration.

4. Re-examine the comprehensive position description of the assistant school principal presented in this chapter. Then make several comparisons between the chapter's position description and the assistant principal's responsibilities at your school or in a school with which you are most familiar. What are the results?

CASE STUDIES

Case 6.1 The Case of the Company Volunteers

Reliable Chemical Company
Office of the Manager
Madison, Lafayette

Emery Sorensen, Assistant Principal
Wymore High School
Madison, Lafayette
October 2

Dear Assistant Principal Sorensen
In accordance with our policy of community cooperation, we wish to inaugurate a new program of assistance to the school systems in the Wymore community. I first called Principal Rodriquez and he kindly referred me to you indicating that you were handling program services.

What we are willing to do is to put a number of our chemists, engineers, and technicians at your disposal for a period of time from 9:30 a.m. to 12:30 p.m. for presentations and labs on modern scientific developments, keyed to the high school student.

It is our feeling that programs of this sort will enhance the science programs offered in the participating high schools and encourage students to consider careers in science fields.

We hope to have programs underway by January 15 of next year. Therefore, it would be appreciated if you would let me know if your high school would be interested in participating.

Thank you for your attention to this request.

Truly Yours,
George W. Jacks

Questions

1. Assume the role of Assistant Principal Sorensen and set forth the administrative procedures/steps that you will take in response to the letter from Mr. Jacks. Don't merely say what you would do, rather perform the administrative activities that you would actually perform in view of the information that you have on hand at this time. For example, if you would write a letter, rather than tell us that you would write a letter actually write the letter that you plan to send, make the calls that you would complete, contact the individuals that you would contact and indicate what you will say or request.

2. Using the compendium of tasks, competencies and indicators listed in this chapter, identify each one that would apply to your administrative procedures.

3. Estimate the time that your activities will take.

4. What priority will you give this request?

References

Baird, L., Meshoulam, I., & DeGive, G. (1983). Meshing human resources planning with strategic business planning: A model approach. *Personnel*, 60(5), 14–25.

Campbell, R.F., & Gregg, R.T. (1957). *Administrative behavior in education.* New York: Harper & Brothers.

Douglass, H.R. (1951). The 1950 revision of the Douglass high school teaching load formula. *NASSP Bulletin*, 35, 13–14.

Goetz, B.E. (1949). *Management planning and control: A managerial approach to industrial accounting.* New York: McGraw-Hill.

Hanlon, J.M. (1968). *Administration and education.* Belmont, CA: Wadsworth.

Human Resources Systems Group Ltd. (HRSG) (2013). Competency-based talent management. From the web: www.competencycore.com/why-competency-based-talent-management

Koontz, H., & O'Donnell, C. (1972). *Principles of management: An analysis of managerial functions.* New York: McGraw-Hill.

Laurence, P.R., & Lorsch, J.W. (1967). Differentiation and integration in complex organizations. *Administration and Science Quarterly*, 12(1), 1–47.

Mathews, J., Debolt, D., & Percival, D. (2014). 10 time management tips that work. From the web: www.entrepreneur.com/article/219553

Morgan, G. (1987). *Images of organization.* Newbury Park, CA: Sage.

Norton, M.S. (2008). *Human resources administration for educational leaders.* Thousand Oaks, CA: Sage.

Norton, M.S., & Bria, R. (1992). Toward an equitable measure of elementary school teacher load. *Record in Educational Administration and Supervision*, 13(1), 62–66.

Pfeiffer, J.W., Goodstein, L.D., & Nolan, T.M. (1986). Applied strategic planning: A new model for strategic growth and vitality. In J.W. Pfeiffer (Ed.), *Strategic planning: Selected readings* (pp. 1–25). San Diego, CA: University Associates.

Taylor, F.W. (1911). *The principles of scientific management.* New York: Harper & Row.

U.S. News and World Report (December 3, 1973). How to make the most of your time. Interview with R. Alec MacKenzie.

Young, I.P. (2008). *The human resource function in educational administration.* 9th ed. Upper Saddle River, NJ: Pearson Merrill Prentice Hall.

Index

Made in the USA
Lexington, KY
03 January 2017